PASTA MAKING

Welcome to Pasta World

(Pasta Cookbook With Easy Recipes & Fresh Pasta)

Jewel Pruett

Published by Alex Howard

© Jewel Pruett
All Rights Reserved

Pasta Making: Welcome to Pasta World (Pasta Cookbook With Easy Recipes & Fresh Pasta)

ISBN 978-1-990169-06-9

All rights reserved. No part of this guide may be reproduced in any form without permission in writing from the publisher except in the case of brief quotations embodied in critical articles or reviews.

Legal & Disclaimer

The information contained in this book is not designed to replace or take the place of any form of medicine or professional medical advice. The information in this book has been provided for educational and entertainment purposes only.

The information contained in this book has been compiled from sources deemed reliable, and it is accurate to the best of the Author's knowledge; however, the Author cannot guarantee its accuracy and validity and cannot be held liable for any errors or omissions. Changes are periodically made to this book. You must consult your doctor or get professional medical advice before using any of the suggested remedies, techniques, or information in this book.

Table of contents

PART 1 1

INTRODUCTION 2

CREAMY PASTA SAUCES 3

Alfredo Sauce 3
Better Than Olive Garden Alfredo Sauce 4
Buttery Alfredo Sauce 6
Cajun Shrimp Alfredo 8
Chicken Broccoli and Spinach Alfredo 9
Classic Alfredo Sauce 11
Cream Cheese Alfredo Sauce 13
Easy Alfredo Sauce I 14
Easy Alfredo Sauce II 15
Easy Alfredo Sauce III 16
Easy Vegan Cauliflower Alfredo Sauce 17
.... 18
GlutenFree Alfredo Sauce 18
Hacked Alfredo Sauce 20
Ham and Asparagus Fettuccine 21
Healthier Alfredo Sauce 22
Healthier Quick and Easy Alfredo Sauce 23
Homemade Chicken Fettuccine 24
Jalapeno Rosemary Alfredo 26
Lemon Basil Alfredo Sauce 27
Lighter Chicken Fettuccine Alfredo 28
Paleo Alfredo Sauce 30
Pumpkin Alfredo Sauce 31
Quick Alfredo Sauce 33
Quick and Easy Alfredo Sauce 34
Simple Garlic and Black Pepper Sauce 35
Skinny Alfredo Sauce 37
Smoked Salmon Alfredo Sauce 38

Smoked Salmon and Artichoke in Alfredo Sauce 40
Spinach Alfredo Sauce Better than Olive Garden 41
Tomato Alfredo Sauce with Artichokes 42
Vegan Alfredo Sauce 43

DELICIOUS & CREAMY SAUCES 45

Almond Sauce Chicken Breasts 45
Asparagus with OrangeCream Sauce and Cashews 47
Basic Bechamel Sauce 49
Basil Cream Sauce 50
Bechamel Sauce 51
Blender Bearnaise Sauce 52
BLT Pasta Carbonara 54
Cajun Ponchartrain Sauce 56
Chef Johns Penne with Vodka Sauce 58
Chef Johns White Sauce 60
Chipotle Chile and Blue Cheese Sauce 62
Crab Cake Sauce 62
Creamy Alfredo Sauce 63
Creamy Pumpkin Sauce 65
Easy Vodka Sauce 67
Eggplant Fillets with Cream Sauce 68
Four Cheese Sauce 69
Fresh Fig and Prosciutto Pasta Sauce 70
Garlic Sauce with Broccoli and Bacon 71
GarlicTarragon Cream Sauce 73
Gorgonzola Sauce 74
Lobster Sauce for Mashed Potatoes 75
Mango Cream Sauce 77
Mushroom Cream Sauce With Shallots 78
Mussels in Curry Cream Sauce 79
Nicks Pepper Sauce Sauce au Poivre 80
NoCook Cashew Alfredo 81
Pink Sauce for Pasta Shrimp 82
Pressure Cooker Creamy Cauliflower Cheese Sauce 84

Pumpkin Ravioli with Creamy Crab Sauce	85
Roasted Garlic Peppercorn Sauce	87
Roasted Red Pepper Cream Sauce	88
Seafood Wine Sauc	89
Simple Lobster Scampi	91
Smoked Salmon Vodka Cream Sauce	92
Spicy Shrimp in Cream Sauce	93
TomatoCream Sauce for Pasta	94
Vodka Sauce	96
White Cheese Sauce	98
White Cream Sauce	98
White Pizza Sauce	99
White Sauce for Pasta	100
White Sauce with Ham and Herbs	102
White Wine and Mushroom Sauce	104

TASTY PASTA RECIPES 106

1) Farfalle with Creamy Wild Mushroom Sauce	106
2) Shrimp Fra Diavolo	108
3) Fettuccine Alfredo with Bacon	109
4) Cavatappi with Bacon and Summer Vegetables	111
5) Baked Ziti and Summer Veggies	112
7) Peppery Chicken Pasta Salad	115
10) Peppery Monterey Jack Pasta Salad	119
11) Zucchini Fusilli	120
12) Quick-Roasted Cherry Tomato Sauce with Spaghetti	122
13) Pasta with Asparagus, Pancetta, and Pine Nuts	124
14) Roasted Butternut Squash and Bacon Pasta	126
15) Orecchiette with Peas, Shrimp, and Buttermilk-Herb Dressing	127
16) Sausage, Tomato, and Arugula Fettuccine	129
17) Bow Ties with Tomatoes, Feta, and Balsamic Dressing	131
18) Whole-Wheat Spaghetti with Arugula	133
19) Roasted Asparagus and Tomato Penne Salad with Goat Cheese	134
20) Farfalle with Tomatoes, Onions, and Spinach	135
21) Mushroom Bolognese	138

22) Wax Bean, Roasted Pepper, and Tomato Pasta with Goat Cheese 139
23) Asparagus and Chicken Carbonara 141
24) Penne with Sausage, Eggplant, and Feta 143

PART 2 145

1) Classic Tomato Pasta Sauce 146
2) Friulano Cheese & Sour Cream Pasta Sauce 148
3) Vodka & Ham Pasta Sauce 149
4) Kalamata Olive & Red Pepper Pasta Sauce 151
5) Bacon & Worcester Pasta Sauce 152
6) Half-and-Half & Butternut Squash Pasta Sauce 154
7) Green Herbs & Cheese Pasta Sauce 155
8) Anchovy, Tomatoes & Olives Pasta Sauce (Puttanesca) 156
9) Cheese, Nutmeg & Whipping Cream Pasta Sauce (Alfredo) 157
10) Mushroom & Bell Pepper Pasta Sauce 158
11) Multi Veggie Pasta Sauce (Primavera) 160
12) Jarlsberg, Bocconcini & Blue Cheese Pasta Sauce 162
13) Artichoke & Lemon Pasta Sauce 163
14) Broccoli & Garlic Pasta Sauce 164
15) Chili Prawns Pasta Sauce 165
16) Herbs & White Bean Pasta Sauce 167
17) Capers & Tuna Pasta Sauce 169
18) White wine & Clam Pasta Sauce 171
19) Eggs, French Beans & Vinaigrette Pasta Sauce (Niçoise) 173
20) Lime, Cream & Tequila Pasta Sauce 174
21) Olive oil & Garlic Pasta Sauce 176
22) Beef & Celery Pasta Sauce 177
23) Spinach & Parmesan Pasta Sauce 179
24) Sea Food Pasta Sauce 180
25) Honey & Peanut Butter Pasta Sauce 182
26) Bechamel Pasta Sauce 183
27) Italian Sausage & Basil Pasta Sauce 185
28) Bolognese Pasta Sauce 186
29) Peppercorn Pasta Sauce 187
30) Butter, Herbs & White Wine Pasta Sauce 189

31) Cream, Stock, Cheese & White wine Pasta Sauce 190

Part 1

Introduction

For many people, side dishes play just a minor role in a meal. However, they're good for your health as long as you pick the right side dishes. Since their ingredients are mostly fruits and veggies, they have fewer calories than main dishes do. Side dishes help prevent many health problems, including cancers and heart disease.

Making yummy pasta sauce will take you just a few minutes. Save more time by preparing a side dish while you're cooking the main dish.

Don't worry if the veggies in your fridge go to bed. Simply follow our pasta sauce recipes to come up with great dishes everyone will love.

Keep In Touch.

You also see more different types of side dish recipes such as:
- Sauces & Condiments
- Side Dish for Two
- Thanksgiving Side Dishes
- Diabetic Side Dishes
- Italian Side Dish
- ...

Let's live happily and cook yourself every day!

Enjoy the book,

Creamy Pasta Sauces

Alfredo Sauce

"Rich and creamy! I have found that Parmesan cheese doesn't melt well, and often substitute Gruyere cheese."

Serving: 4 | Prep: 10 m | Cook: 10 m | Ready in: 20 m
Ingredients

- 1/4 cup butter
- 1 cup heavy cream
- 1 clove garlic, crushed
- 1 1/2 cups freshly grated Parmesan cheese
- 1/4 cup chopped fresh parsley

Direction

- Melt butter in a medium saucepan over medium low heat. Add cream and simmer for 5 minutes, then add garlic and cheese and whisk quickly, heating through. Stir in parsley and serve.

Nutrition Information

- Calories: 439 calories
- Total Fat: 42.1 g
- Cholesterol: 138 mg
- Sodium: 565 mg
- Total Carbohydrate: 3.4 g
- Protein: 13 g

Better Than Olive Garden Alfredo Sauce

"Whether it's chicken Alfredo or fettuccine Alfredo, the Alfredo sauce has always had my heart. This is a simple and basic recipe for Italian starters. Enjoy!"

Serving: 4 | Prep: 10 m | Cook: 20 m | Ready in: 30 m
Ingredients

- 3 tablespoons sweet butter
- 2 tablespoons olive oil
- 2 cups heavy whipping cream
- 2 cloves garlic, minced
- 1/4 teaspoon ground white pepper

- 1/2 cup grated Parmesan cheese
- 3/4 cup shredded mozzarella cheese
- 1 (12 ounce) package angel hair pasta

Direction

- Melt butter and olive oil in a saucepan over medium-low heat. Add cream, garlic, and white pepper; bring to just under a boil. Reduce heat and simmer, stirring often, until mixture is slightly reduced, about 5 minutes.
- Stir Parmesan cheese into cream mixture and simmer until sauce is thickened and smooth, 8 to 10 minutes. Add mozzarella cheese to sauce; cook and stir until cheese is melted, about 5 minutes.
- Bring a large pot of lightly salted water to a boil. Cook angel hair in the boiling water, stirring occasionally until cooked through but firm to the bite, 3 to 5 minutes. Drain and transfer pasta to serving plates. Spoon sauce over pasta.

Nutrition Information

- Calories: 883 calories
- Total Fat: 67.9 g
- Cholesterol: 208 mg
- Sodium: 561 mg
- Total Carbohydrate: 50.8 g
- Protein: 20.5 g

Buttery Alfredo Sauce

"This is a rich, creamy, Italian-style Alfredo sauce perfect for chicken and seafood pastas! I discovered this recipe after relentless searching for an authentic Alfredo sauce that doesn't use cream cheese."

Serving: 8 | Prep: 10 m | Cook: 35 m | Ready in: 45 m

Ingredients

- 1 cup unsalted butter
- 1 1/2 tablespoons minced garlic
- 1 tablespoon all-purpose flour
- 4 cups heavy cream
- 1/4 cup whole milk
- 8 ounces freshly shredded Parmesan cheese
- 2 ounces shredded fontina cheese
- 1/2 teaspoon salt
- 1 teaspoon ground black pepper

Direction

- Melt the butter in a large pot over medium heat. Stir in the garlic and flour, and cook and stir until the garlic is fragrant but not browned, about 1 minute. Whisk in heavy cream and milk, whisking constantly until the mixture is hot and slightly thickened, about 10 minutes. Gradually stir in the Parmesan cheese and fontina cheese. Season with salt and black pepper. Continue to simmer until the cheese has melted and the sauce is thickened, stirring often, 20 to 30 more minutes.

Nutrition Information

- Calories: 771 calories
- Total Fat: 77.3 g
- Cholesterol: 253 mg
- Sodium: 736 mg
- Total Carbohydrate: 6.2 g
- Protein: 15.7 g

Cajun Shrimp Alfredo

"Spicy and creamy....a great combination! Homemade Alfredo is always best, but the Knorr® mix plus Parmesan is a quick easy alternative. Serve over angel hair pasta."

Serving: 6 | Prep: 20 m | Cook: 15 m | Ready in: 35 m
Ingredients

- 1/2 pound andouille sausage, diced
- 1/4 onion, diced
- 1/4 cup diced celery
- 1/4 cup diced red bell pepper
- 2 teaspoons Cajun seasoning
- 1/4 teaspoon dried sage
- 1 pound raw shrimp, peeled and deveined
- 1 3/4 cups milk
- 1 (1.6 oz) package dry Alfredo sauce mix (such as Knorr®)
- 1 tablespoon butter
- 1/2 cup freshly grated Parmesan cheese
- 2 teaspoons minced garlic, divided

Direction

- Combine sausage, onion, celery, red bell pepper, Cajun seasoning, and sage in a skillet; cook and stir until sausage is cooked through and celery and bell pepper are softened, 5 to 10 minutes. Add shrimp and cook until cooked through and bright pink, about 5 minutes. Remove skillet from heat.

- Whisk milk, Alfredo sauce mix, and butter together in a saucepan; bring to a boil. Reduce heat to low and simmer sauce, stirring occasionally, until smooth and thickened, about 2 minutes. Stir Parmesan cheese and garlic into sauce until cheese is melted. Stir shrimp mixture into sauce.

Nutrition Information

- Calories: 302 calories
- Total Fat: 18.2 g
- Cholesterol: 156 mg
- Sodium: 1148 mg
- Total Carbohydrate: 10.2 g
- Protein: 23.2 g

Chicken Broccoli and Spinach Alfredo

"Verrrry creamy and filling perfect for a family meal. Serve with Parmesan cheese and a loaf of crusty bread."

Serving: 4 | Prep: 15 m | Cook: 28 m | Ready in: 43 m

Ingredients

- 1 (12 ounce) package linguine pasta
- 2 1/2 cups chopped broccoli florets
- 10 slices bacon
- 1/4 cup boiling water
- 4 cubes chicken bouillon
- 1 cup sliced fresh mushrooms
- 6 cloves garlic, minced

- 4 skinless, boneless chicken breast, cut into bite-size pieces
- 1 (8 ounce) package cream cheese, softened
- 3/4 cup milk
- 1/2 cup grated Parmesan cheese
- 1/2 teaspoon dried basil
- 1/2 teaspoon dried parsley
- 2 cups fresh baby spinach

Direction

- Bring a large pot of lightly salted water to a boil. Cook linguine at a boil until almost tender, about 9 minutes. Add broccoli; continue cooking until linguine is tender, about 2 minutes more. Drain.
- Place bacon in a large skillet and cook over medium-high heat, turning occasionally, until evenly browned, about 10 minutes. Drain bacon slices on paper towels. Drain grease.
- Combine boiling water and chicken bouillon cubes in a bowl; mix until dissolved.
- Pour chicken bouillon mixture into the same skillet used to cook the bacon. Bring to a simmer. Add mushrooms and garlic; cook for 1 minute. Add chicken; cook and stir until no longer pink in the center, about 5 minutes. Stir in cream cheese, milk, Parmesan cheese, basil, and parsley; cook until melted together and heated through, about 5 minutes.
- Place spinach in a microwave-safe bowl. Fill bowl halfway with water. Cook in the microwave until wilted, about 2 minutes.

- Stir wilted spinach into the cooked linguine. Pour chicken and sauce on top. Crumble bacon on top.

Nutrition Information

- Calories: 846 calories
- Total Fat: 37.7 g
- Cholesterol: 159 mg
- Sodium: 2106 mg
- Total Carbohydrate: 73.2 g
- Protein: 55 g

Classic Alfredo Sauce

"A satisfying sauce you can use on any type of pasta - dry or fresh."

Serving: 2
Ingredients

- 3 tablespoons butter
- 8 fluid ounces heavy whipping cream
- salt to taste
- 1 pinch ground nutmeg
- 1/4 cup grated Parmesan cheese
- 1/4 cup grated Romano cheese
- 1 egg yolk
- 2 tablespoons grated Parmesan cheese

Direction

- Melt butter or margarine in a saucepan over medium heat. Add heavy cream, stirring constantly. Stir in salt, nutmeg, grated Parmesan cheese, and grated Romano cheese. Stir constantly until melted, then mix in egg yolk. Simmer over medium low heat for 3 to 5 minutes. Garnish with additional grated Parmesan cheese, if desired.

Nutrition Information

- Calories: 714 calories
- Total Fat: 72 g
- Cholesterol: 340 mg
- Sodium: 580 mg
- Total Carbohydrate: 5 g
- Protein: 14.5 g

Cream Cheese Alfredo Sauce

"This is my spin on Alfredo sauce. We love cream cheese, mushrooms and garlic. So I decided to try different ways of creating this tasty dish! Serve with fettuccini, and sliced crusty bread for mopping!"

Serving: 6 | Prep: 10 m | Cook: 15 m | Ready in: 25 m

Ingredients

- 2 tablespoons butter
- 2 portobello mushroom caps, thinly sliced
- 1 (8 ounce) package cream cheese
- 1/2 cup butter
- 1 1/2 cups milk
- 6 ounces grated Parmesan cheese, or to taste
- 1 clove garlic, crushed
- 1 tablespoon minced fresh basil leaves
- ground white pepper, to taste

Direction

- Heat 2 tablespoons of butter in a skillet over medium heat. Stir in the mushrooms; cook and stir until softened, about 5 minutes. Set aside.
- Meanwhile, melt the cream cheese and 1/2 cup of butter in a saucepan over medium heat, stirring occasionally. Stir in the milk and Parmesan cheese, mixing until smooth. Add in the garlic, basil, and white pepper. Simmer for 5 minutes, then remove the garlic. Stir in the cooked mushrooms before serving.

Nutrition Information

- Calories: 464 calories
- Total Fat: 41.6 g
- Cholesterol: 122 mg
- Sodium: 708 mg
- Total Carbohydrate: 7.2 g
- Protein: 16.9 g

Easy Alfredo Sauce I

"This is a quick and easy side dish, that my family loves with chicken!"

Serving: 8 | Cook: 15 m | Ready in: 15 m
Ingredients

- 1 pint heavy whipping cream
- 1/2 cup butter
- 1 1/2 cups grated Parmesan cheese

Direction

- In a medium saucepan combine whipping cream, butter or margarine, and grated Parmesan cheese. Cook over medium low heat until smooth. Remove from heat. Sauce will thicken upon standing.

Nutrition Information

- Calories: 372 calories
- Total Fat: 37.8 g
- Cholesterol: 125 mg
- Sodium: 334 mg
- Total Carbohydrate: 2.3 g

- Protein: 7.1 g

Easy Alfredo Sauce II

"This recipe for Fettuccine Alfredo is so easy and delicious that my family requests it constantly! We like this best served with grilled chicken breasts and broccoli or spinach. If you are lucky enough to have any left over, you can mix them together for a feast the next day. Enjoy!"

Serving: 8 | Prep: 5 m | Ready in: 5 m
Ingredients

- 1/2 cup butter, room temperature
- 3/4 cup grated Parmesan cheese
- 1 cup heavy cream

Direction

- In a medium bowl, beat butter and Parmesan with an electric mixer until fluffy. Add cream, a little at a time, until mixture resembles softly scrambled eggs. Toss with hot pasta to serve.

Nutrition Information

- Calories: 237 calories
- Total Fat: 24.7 g
- Cholesterol: 78 mg
- Sodium: 208 mg
- Total Carbohydrate: 1.1 g
- Protein: 3.6 g

Easy Alfredo Sauce III

"This recipe is enough for about one pound of pasta. Enjoy!"

Serving: 4 | Cook: 15 m | Ready in: 15 m
Ingredients

- 1 cup half-and-half cream
- 1 cup whole milk
- 2 egg yolks, beaten
- 2 cups grated Parmesan cheese
- salt and pepper to taste

Direction

- In a medium saucepan over medium heat, combine half-and-half and milk. Heat through, then reduce heat to low and stir in egg yolks and cheese, a little at a time, until well incorporated. Simmer 5 to 10 minutes, until thick, stirring occasionally. Stir in salt and pepper to taste and toss with hot pasta.

Nutrition Information

- Calories: 314 calories
- Total Fat: 22.6 g
- Cholesterol: 166 mg
- Sodium: 665 mg
- Total Carbohydrate: 7.3 g
- Protein: 20.5 g

Easy Vegan Cauliflower Alfredo Sauce

"Make this quick and easy cauliflower-based vegan Alfredo sauce, so rich, and creamy, completely dairy-free, and keto-friendly as well!"

Serving: 4 | Prep: 13 m | Cook: 9 m | Ready in: 22 m

Ingredients

- 1 teaspoon olive oil
- 1/2 white onion, chopped
- 3 cloves garlic, crushed
- 3 cups chopped cauliflower
- 1 cup vegetable broth
- 1 tablespoon nutritional yeast
- 2 teaspoons Himalayan salt
- 1 1/2 teaspoons lemon juice
- 1/2 teaspoon soy sauce

Direction

- Heat olive oil in a saucepan over medium heat. Add onion and cook until soft, about 3 minutes. Add garlic and cook for 1 minute more. Add cauliflower and vegetable broth; cover with lid and simmer over medium heat until tender, about 5 minutes.
- Place cauliflower mixture in a blender. Add nutritional yeast, salt, lemon juice, and soy sauce; blend until smooth and creamy, about 3 minutes.

Nutrition Information

- Calories: 28 calories
- Total Fat: 1.4 g
- Cholesterol: 0 mg
- Sodium: 1316 mg
- Total Carbohydrate: 2.8 g
- Protein: 1.4 g

GlutenFree Alfredo Sauce

"This is a gluten-free Alfredo sauce. It can be used as a pasta sauce, a topping for baked potatoes, or a sauce for pizza."

Serving: 2 | Prep: 5 m | Cook: 10 m | Ready in: 15 m
Ingredients

- 3 tablespoons butter
- 1/2 cup heavy cream
- 1 1/2 cups freshly grated Parmesan cheese
- 1/4 teaspoon garlic powder
- 2 pinches freshly grated nutmeg, or to taste
- freshly ground black pepper to taste
- chopped fresh parsley, or to taste (optional)

Direction

- Melt butter in a heavy saucepan over medium heat. Slowly add cream, stirring until well combined, about 3 minutes. Add Parmesan cheese; cook and stir until well incorporated, about 3 minutes. Stir in garlic powder, nutmeg, and black pepper and cook for 2 minutes. Serve sprinkled with fresh parsley.

Nutrition Information

- Calories: 624 calories
- Total Fat: 56.8 g
- Cholesterol: 180 mg
- Sodium: 1064 mg
- Total Carbohydrate: 5.2 g
- Protein: 24.7 g

Hacked Alfredo Sauce

"I wanted to make an Alfredo sauce for a pasta dish, but didn't have a lot on hand (no butter or heavy cream). Here is my hacked version, which is probably a lot less fattening than a classic Alfredo. Play around with it and with what you have on hand. I used this sauce in the Spicy Sausage Alfredo dish I also posted on the site."

Serving: 4 | Prep: 10 m | Cook: 10 m | Ready in: 20 m
Ingredients

- 2 tablespoons olive oil
- 2 tablespoons all-purpose flour
- 2 cloves garlic, minced
- 3 tablespoons chopped fresh parsley
- 1 1/2 cups 2% milk
- 2 ounces cream cheese
- 1/4 cup Parmesan cheese
- 2 tablespoons half-and-half
- salt and ground black pepper to taste

Direction

- Heat olive oil in a saucepan over medium-high heat. Stir in flour until a light paste forms, 1 to 2 minutes. Add garlic; cook and stir until fragrant, about 1 minute. Stir in parsley.
- Whisk milk slowly into the saucepan. Bring sauce to a simmer; cook until slightly thickened, about 5 minutes. Reduce heat and whisk in cream cheese,

Parmesan cheese, and half-and-half until smooth. Season with salt and black pepper.

Nutrition Information

- Calories: 205 calories
- Total Fat: 15.9 g
- Cholesterol: 30 mg
- Sodium: 200 mg
- Total Carbohydrate: 8.8 g
- Protein: 6.8 g

Ham and Asparagus Fettuccine

"I LOVE fettuccine, and when made with a bit of leftover ham it takes on a heartiness and richness so filling there isn't room for dessert!"

Serving: 6 | Prep: 5 m | Cook: 15 m | Ready in: 20 m

Ingredients

- 12 ounces dry fettuccini noodles
- 8 ounces fresh asparagus, trimmed and cut into 2 inch pieces
- 1/2 cup butter
- 2 cups heavy cream
- 3/4 cup grated Parmesan cheese
- 1/4 teaspoon garlic powder
- 1/4 teaspoon ground black pepper
- 1 pinch cayenne pepper
- 1/2 pound cooked ham, diced

Direction

- Bring a large pot of lightly salted water to a boil. Add pasta and cook for 8 to 10 minutes or until al dente. Stir asparagus into pot in the last five minutes of cooking; drain.
- While pasta is cooking, heat butter and cream in a medium saucepan over medium heat. When mixture begins to bubble, stir in Parmesan, garlic powder, pepper and cayenne. Continue cooking until mixture thickens, stirring occasionally. Stir in ham and heat through.
- Toss pasta and asparagus with sauce and serve immediately.

Nutrition Information

- Calories: 754 calories
- Total Fat: 55.9 g
- Cholesterol: 179 mg
- Sodium: 785 mg
- Total Carbohydrate: 45 g
- Protein: 20.9 g

Healthier Alfredo Sauce

"Zucchini provides a healthy touch to this delightfully rich and creamy sauce! Reduced amounts of cream and cheese also make this great recipe healthier."

Serving: 4 | Prep: 15 m | Cook: 10 m | Ready in: 25 m
Ingredients

- 1 pound whole wheat fettuccine

- 8 ounces zucchini, cut into thin strips with a vegetable peeler
- 2 tablespoons butter
- 1 clove garlic, crushed
- 1/2 cup heavy cream
- 1 cup freshly grated Parmesan cheese
- 1/4 cup chopped fresh parsley

Direction

- Fill a large pot with lightly salted water and bring to a rolling boil. Stir in the fettuccine, bring back to a boil, and cook pasta over medium heat until cooked through but still firm to the bite, about 8 minutes. Lightly cook zucchini by tossing into pasta water just before draining.
- Heat butter and garlic in a saucepan over medium-low heat. Stir in cream and simmer for 5 minutes, then add cheese and whisk quickly, heating through. Stir in parsley.
- Toss sauce with cooked whole wheat fettuccine and zucchini strips.

Nutrition Information

- Calories: 251 calories
- Total Fat: 22.6 g
- Cholesterol: 74 mg
- Sodium: 366 mg
- Total Carbohydrate: 4 g
- Protein: 9.2 g

Healthier Quick and Easy Alfredo Sauce

"This alfredo is great just a little lighter than before. Not as rich but still so tasty. Great when served with whole wheat noodles."

Serving: 4 | Prep: 5 m | Cook: 5 m | Ready in: 10 m

Ingredients

- 1/4 cup butter
- 1 (8 ounce) package fat-free cream cheese
- 2 teaspoons garlic powder
- 2 cups non-fat milk
- 6 ounces grated Parmesan cheese
- 1/8 teaspoon ground black pepper

Direction

- Melt butter in a non-stick saucepan over medium heat; melt cream cheese and garlic powder in butter, whisking Pour in milk, a little at a time, whisking to smooth out lumps. Stir in Parmesan cheese and pepper until smooth.
- Remove from heat when sauce reaches a creamy and thick consistency, about 5 minutes.

Nutrition Information

- Calories: 385 calories
- Total Fat: 24.5 g
- Cholesterol: 75 mg
- Sodium: 1089 mg
- Total Carbohydrate: 12.1 g
- Protein: 28.9 g

Homemade Chicken Fettuccine

"This chicken alfredo recipe is really unique as it doesn't use a thickening agent, and is very versatile!"

Serving: 4 | Prep: 10 m | Cook: 15 m | Ready in: 25 m

Ingredients

- 8 ounces fettuccini pasta
- 2 tablespoons butter
- 3 skinless, boneless chicken breast halves - cut into chunks
- 8 ounces mushrooms, sliced
- 1 teaspoon garlic salt
- 1/8 teaspoon ground black pepper
- 1 1/2 cups heavy cream
- 1/4 cup grated Parmesan cheese

Direction

- Bring a large pot of lightly salted water to a boil. Add fettuccine and cook for 8 to 10 minutes or until al dente; drain.
- In a large skillet, brown chicken and mushrooms in butter until chicken is cooked through. Season with garlic salt and pepper. Add whipping cream and cook until thick, stirring constantly. Add parmesan cheese when at desired consistency. Serve over noodles.

Nutrition Information

- Calories: 791 calories
- Total Fat: 43.9 g
- Cholesterol: 245 mg
- Sodium: 723 mg

- Total Carbohydrate: 46.3 g
- Protein: 53.3 g

Jalapeno Rosemary Alfredo

"A creamy spicy alfredo, great for a dipping sauce!"

Serving: 6 | Prep: 10 m | Cook: 10 m | Ready in: 20 m

Ingredients

- 2 tablespoons olive oil
- 2 cloves garlic, minced
- 1 jalapeno pepper, seeded and minced
- 1 cup heavy cream
- 1/2 cup grated Parmesan cheese
- 1 teaspoon dried rosemary
- 1 pinch salt and ground black pepper to taste

Direction

- Heat the olive oil in a skillet over medium heat. Cook and stir the garlic and jalapeno pepper in the hot oil until fragrant, about 5 minutes; add the heavy cream and bring the mixture to a simmer. Reduce heat to low. Stir the Parmesan cheese and rosemary through the mixture; continue cooking until the cheese is completely melted, about 5 minutes more. Season with salt and pepper to serve.

Nutrition Information

- Calories: 208 calories
- Total Fat: 21.1 g

- Cholesterol: 60 mg
- Sodium: 117 mg
- Total Carbohydrate: 2 g
- Protein: 3.5 g

Lemon Basil Alfredo Sauce

"This creamy sauce draws on Northern Italian ideas for a summer pasta. Experiment to get the taste you want! Great on chicken. Use your favorite noodle that holds sauce."

Serving: 4 | Prep: 10 m | Cook: 45 m | Ready in: 55 m
Ingredients

- 1 (6 ounce) package egg noodles
- 1 lemon, zested
- 1/2 lemon, juiced
- 1/4 cup butter
- 2 cloves garlic, crushed
- 2 cups heavy whipping cream
- 1 cup grated Parmesan cheese
- 1/2 cup grated Romano cheese
- 1/4 cup ricotta cheese
- 2 tablespoons chopped fresh basil, or more to taste
- salt and ground black pepper to taste

Direction

- Bring a large pot of lightly salted water to a boil. Cook egg noodles in the boiling water, stirring occasionally until tender yet firm to the bite, 8 to 10 minutes. Drain.

- Melt butter in a saucepan over medium-low heat, about 2 minutes. Add garlic and cook until simmering, about 1 minute. Add heavy cream. Increase heat to medium and bring to a boil; simmer, stirring occasionally, until Alfredo sauce is reduced by half, about 20 minutes.
- Slowly whisk lemon zest and juice into the Alfredo sauce to avoid curdling. Stir in Parmesan, ricotta, and Romano cheeses until melted, 2 to 3 minutes. Stir in basil, salt, and pepper; cook for 2 to 3 minutes more.
- Pour the Alfredo sauce over the egg noodles.

Nutrition Information

- Calories: 831 calories
- Total Fat: 67.3 g
- Cholesterol: 262 mg
- Sodium: 661 mg
- Total Carbohydrate: 40.1 g
- Protein: 21.7 g

Lighter Chicken Fettuccine Alfredo

"This version of chicken fettuccine alfredo is lightened by substituting some of the heavy cream with chicken broth."

Serving: 6 | Prep: 10 m | Cook: 45 m | Ready in: 1 h 10 m

Ingredients

- 2 large boneless skinless chicken breasts

- 2 cups low-sodium chicken broth
- 4 cloves garlic, minced
- ground black pepper to taste
- 2 cups heavy cream
- 2 egg yolks
- salt to taste
- 1 pound fettuccine
- 1 sprig chopped fresh parsley
- 2 cups freshly grated Parmigiano-Reggiano cheese, divided

Direction

- Combine chicken breasts and chicken broth in a saucepan over medium-high heat. Bring to a boil, cover, and reduce heat to low; simmer for 5 minutes. Turn breasts, cover, and simmer another 5 minutes. Remove from heat and let sit with the cover on for 15 minutes.
- Remove chicken breasts from the broth and set aside to cool, reserving the broth in the saucepan. Once the chicken is cool enough to handle, cut into bite-size slices.
- Return the chicken broth to medium heat and cook until reduced to 1 cup.
- Stir garlic, black pepper, and heavy cream into the reduced broth; bring to a simmer and remove from heat.
- Whisk egg yolks in a bowl until smooth. Beat 1 tablespoon of the warm cream mixture into the

eggs until thoroughly incorporated; repeat until about 1/2 cup of the warm cream mixture is used.
- Whisk the warm cream and egg mixture back into the saucepan with the remaining cream mixture. Cook over medium-low heat, whisking constantly, until the mixture almost comes to a simmer and thickens, about 5 minutes. Season with salt and black pepper to taste.
- Bring a large pot of lightly salted water to a boil. Cook fettuccine in boiling water, stirring occasionally, until nearly cooked through, about 7 minutes. Drain.
- Stir parsley, 1 cup of Parmigiano-Reggiano, and cream mixture into the pasta. Remove from heat, cover, and let sit for a few minutes until thick.
- Fold chicken and 1 cup Parmigiano-Reggiano into the pasta mixture to serve.

Nutrition Information

- Calories: 759 calories
- Total Fat: 41.8 g
- Cholesterol: 239 mg
- Sodium: 505 mg
- Total Carbohydrate: 59.6 g
- Protein: 37.8 g

Paleo Alfredo Sauce

"Delicious. This basic recipe can be used many different ways. Substitute chicken or beef stock for water, add chili powder, chipotle, horseradish, or fresh herbs."

Serving: 2 | Prep: 5 m | Ready in: 20 m
Ingredients

- 1 cup unsalted raw cashews
- 1 1/2 cups boiling water, or more if needed
- 2 tablespoons nutritional yeast
- 2 teaspoons coconut oil
- 1/2 teaspoon garlic salt
- 1/2 teaspoon sea salt, or to taste (optional)
- 1/8 teaspoon ground white pepper

Direction

- Place cashews in a blender; cover with 1 1/2 cups boiling water and let sit for 15 minutes. Add nutritional yeast, coconut oil, garlic salt, sea salt, and pepper; blend until sauce becomes creamy, adding more water if needed.

Nutrition Information

- Calories: 441 calories
- Total Fat: 34.7 g
- Cholesterol: 0 mg
- Sodium: 1050 mg
- Total Carbohydrate: 23.3 g
- Protein: 16.4 g

Pumpkin Alfredo Sauce

"This recipe was a nice way to use up some extra pumpkin we had available. Served it to one person who really enjoys pumpkin (myself) and one who doesn't, and both came away really liking it! Has enough flavor that the pumpkin makes itself known, but not so much that it overpowers the alfredo flavor or texture. Recipe makes enough to toss with one cooked 12 oz. box of pasta."

Serving: 4 | Prep: 5 m | Cook: 10 m | Ready in: 15 m

Ingredients

- 2 tablespoons butter
- 9 sage leaves
- 1 cup heavy whipping cream
- 1 cup pumpkin puree
- 1 teaspoon ground nutmeg
- 1 teaspoon ground cinnamon
- 1 tablespoon grated Parmesan cheese

Direction

- Melt butter in a saucepan over medium heat; cook and stir sage leaves in hot butter until the butter takes on the sage flavor, about 5 minutes.
- Whisk cream, pumpkin, nutmeg, cinnamon, and Parmesan cheese into the butter; cook until the cheese melts, about 5 minutes.

Nutrition Information

- Calories: 289 calories
- Total Fat: 28.6 g
- Cholesterol: 98 mg
- Sodium: 230 mg
- Total Carbohydrate: 7.7 g
- Protein: 2.5 g

Quick Alfredo Sauce

"This alfredo sauce is lower in fat than most, as it is made with half and half. This is delicious over pasta and is easy to make. You can also make it the day before and refrigerate it until ready to use. Serve with a Caesar salad, and you have a delicious meal done in less than an hour."

Serving: 8 | Prep: 10 m | Cook: 5 m | Ready in: 15 m

Ingredients

- 1/4 cup butter
- 1/4 cup all-purpose flour
- 1/2 teaspoon garlic salt
- 2 cups half and half
- 2 cloves garlic, minced
- 1 tablespoon dried parsley flakes
- 1/3 cup grated Parmesan cheese

Direction

- Melt the butter in a saucepan over medium heat. Whisk the flour and garlic salt into the melted butter until the mixture is smooth. Slowly beat the half and half into the sauce until completely incorporated. Stir the garlic, parsley, and Parmesan cheese into the sauce, whisking continually. Bring the sauce to a simmer; cook, stirring regularly, until the sauce has thickened, 4 to 5 minutes. Use immediately or refrigerate.

Nutrition Information

- Calories: 160 calories
- Total Fat: 13.7 g
- Cholesterol: 41 mg
- Sodium: 231 mg
- Total Carbohydrate: 6.1 g
- Protein: 3.6 g

Quick and Easy Alfredo Sauce

"I experimented with this until I found a quick, cheap, and easy Alfredo sauce combination -- the secret is cream cheese!"

Serving: 4 | Prep: 5 m | Cook: 5 m | Ready in: 10 m
Ingredients

- 1/2 cup butter
- 1 (8 ounce) package cream cheese
- 2 teaspoons garlic powder
- 2 cups milk
- 6 ounces grated Parmesan cheese
- 1/8 teaspoon ground black pepper

Direction

- Melt butter in a medium, non-stick saucepan over medium heat. Add cream cheese and garlic powder, stirring with wire whisk until smooth. Add milk, a little at a time, whisking to smooth out lumps. Stir in Parmesan and pepper. Remove from heat when sauce reaches desired consistency. Sauce will thicken rapidly, thin with milk if cooked too long. Toss with hot pasta to serve.

Nutrition Information

- Calories: 648 calories
- Total Fat: 57.1 g
- Cholesterol: 170 mg
- Sodium: 1030 mg
- Total Carbohydrate: 10 g
- Protein: 25.1 g

Simple Garlic and Black Pepper Sauce

"A simple pasta sauce using a few common ingredients, this is kind of like an Alfredo, but not nearly as rich. It's very light and flavorful and pretty low in fat, depending on what kind of milk you use. I made this up because I didn't have any butter for my kids' noodles, and dry noodles just won't do!"

Serving: 4 | Prep: 10 m | Cook: 6 m | Ready in: 16 m

Ingredients

- 1/4 cup olive oil
- 2 tablespoons minced garlic, or more to taste
- 1 1/2 cups 2% milk
- 1 teaspoon salt
- 1 teaspoon ground black pepper
- 2 teaspoons water
- 1/2 teaspoon cornstarch

Direction

- Heat olive oil in a saucepan over medium-low heat. Add garlic, cook and stir until fragrant, 1 to 2

minutes. Add milk, salt, and pepper; stir constantly until simmering, about 2 minutes.
- Whisk water and cornstarch together in a bowl until smooth. Add water-cornstarch mixture to sauce; stir continuously until sauce is thickened to desired consistency, 3 to 5 minutes.

Nutrition Information

- Calories: 174 calories
- Total Fat: 15.3 g
- Cholesterol: 7 mg
- Sodium: 620 mg
- Total Carbohydrate: 6.3 g
- Protein: 3.3 g

Skinny Alfredo Sauce

"This is a skinny version of everyone's favorite Alfredo sauce. You won't miss the cream or butter one bit!"

Serving: 4 | Prep: 5 m | Cook: 15 m | Ready in: 20 m

Ingredients

- 1 tablespoon grapeseed oil
- 1 tablespoon minced garlic
- 1 tablespoon all-purpose flour
- 1 cup chicken broth
- 1 cup fat-free milk
- 2/3 cup grated Parmesan cheese
- 1/2 teaspoon salt
- 1/4 teaspoon ground black pepper

Direction

- Heat oil in a saucepan over medium heat. Add garlic; cook and stir until golden, about 1 minute. Mix in flour and cook until you have a thick paste, about 1 minute. Whisk chicken broth in slowly until mixture is smooth, about 2 minutes. Pour in milk and whisk until smooth.
- Simmer mixture until thick, about 10 minutes. Add Parmesan cheese, salt, and pepper; stir until cheese melts and sauce is smooth.

Nutrition Information

- Calories: 123 calories
- Total Fat: 7.4 g
- Cholesterol: 13 mg

- Sodium: 531 mg
- Total Carbohydrate: 6.2 g
- Protein: 7.9 g

Smoked Salmon Alfredo Sauce

"Can be served with fettuccine, linguine, or penne."

Serving: 4 | Prep: 10 m | Cook: 30 m | Ready in: 40 m
Ingredients

- 1/4 onion, chopped
- 1/4 cup butter
- 1/2 pound smoked salmon, chopped
- 1 pint heavy whipping cream
- 1 tomato, diced
- 2 tablespoons chopped fresh parsley
- ground black pepper to taste

Direction

- Sauté onion in the butter in a pan until clear. Add the salmon and sauté at medium to low heat for approximately 2 more minutes. Very gradually, start to add the cream. Stir constantly until thickened. Sauce should be very thick once you have added all the cream. Top with tomato and parsley; season with pepper.

Nutrition Information

- Calories: 588 calories
- Total Fat: 58.1 g
- Cholesterol: 207 mg

- Sodium: 575 mg
- Total Carbohydrate: 5.5 g
- Protein: 13.4 g

Smoked Salmon and Artichoke in Alfredo Sauce

"I first tasted this delicious recipe while visiting a northern California coast micro brewery. This is my version. Serve over linguine and garnish with parsley and additional Parmesan cheese."

Serving: 8 | Prep: 15 m | Cook: 25 m | Ready in: 40 m
Ingredients

- 2 tablespoons butter
- 2 tablespoons extra-virgin olive oil
- 2 cups coarsely chopped onions
- salt and ground black pepper to taste
- 4 cloves garlic, coarsely chopped
- 1 (14 ounce) can artichoke hearts, drained and quartered
- 1 cup white wine
- 1 cup chicken broth
- 2 tablespoons lemon juice
- 2 teaspoons lemon zest
- 1/4 teaspoon red pepper flakes
- 3/4 pound smoked salmon, cut into small pieces
- 1 cup heavy whipping cream
- 1/2 cup grated Parmesan cheese

Direction

- Heat butter and olive oil together in a large skillet over medium heat; cook and stir onion and salt until

translucent, 5 to 10 minutes. Add garlic and cook until fragrant, about 1 minute. Reduce heat to medium-low; add artichoke hearts, wine, chicken broth, lemon juice, lemon zest and red pepper flakes; simmer until liquid is reduced and thickened into a sauce, about 10 minutes.
- Mix salmon, cream, Parmesan cheese, salt, and pepper into sauce; simmer until thickened, about 5 minutes.

Nutrition Information

- Calories: 293 calories
- Total Fat: 20.7 g
- Cholesterol: 63 mg
- Sodium: 767 mg
- Total Carbohydrate: 9.9 g
- Protein: 12.1 g

Spinach Alfredo Sauce Better than Olive Garden

"Better than Olive Garden®! Top with grilled chicken on fettuccine pasta for a complete meal or use as a dip for bread sticks. Delicious rich and creamy spinach Alfredo everyone will love. When I make this dish, everyone raves over it! Add more spinach if you're a spinach lover or leave it out if you're not a fan. I like adding lots of garlic! For a thicker sauce, add more cream cheese."

Serving: 5 | Prep: 10 m | Cook: 15 m | Ready in: 25 m
Ingredients

- 1/2 cup butter
- 3/4 cup thawed frozen chopped spinach
- 1 pint heavy whipping cream
- 3 tablespoons cream cheese
- 1 cup grated Parmesan cheese
- 1 teaspoon garlic powder
- 1 pinch salt and ground black pepper to taste (optional)

Direction

- Heat butter in a saucepan over low heat; cook spinach in the melted butter until warmed, about 1 minute. Add cream and cream cheese to spinach mixture; cook and stir until cream cheese is melted, about 5 minutes.
- Fold Parmesan cheese and garlic powder into spinach mixture; season with salt and pepper. Simmer until sauce is thickened and smooth, about 10 more minutes.

Nutrition Information

- Calories: 599 calories
- Total Fat: 61.4 g
- Cholesterol: 203 mg
- Sodium: 455 mg
- Total Carbohydrate: 4.9 g
- Protein: 9.9 g

Tomato Alfredo Sauce with Artichokes

"Less rich than the usual Alfredo sauce. Delicious!"

Serving: 5

Ingredients

- 1 (14 ounce) can artichoke hearts in water
- 2 tomatoes, chopped
- 1 onion, chopped
- 1 cup fresh sliced mushrooms
- 1/2 cup chopped fresh basil
- 1/2 cup whole milk
- 2 tablespoons all-purpose flour

Direction

- Chop artichoke hearts and place in large skillet with juice. Thicken with flour and milk to desired consistency.
- Add onion, mushrooms, tomatoes, and basil. Cook for a short time, leaving vegetables firm and tasty and pretty.
- Cook up a batch of your favorite spaghetti noodles (e.g., angel hair or spaghettini). Rinse. Toss artichoke sauce on top of cooked pasta.

Nutrition Information

- Calories: 90 calories
- Total Fat: 1 g
- Cholesterol: 2 mg
- Sodium: 490 mg
- Total Carbohydrate: 16.4 g
- Protein: 5.1 g

Vegan Alfredo Sauce

"Vegan Alfredo sauce you can just pour over your favorite pasta."

Serving: 2 | Prep: 5 m | Ready in: 5 m
Ingredients

- 3 ounces shredded mozzarella-style vegan cheese (such as Daiya®)
- 1/4 cup soy milk
- 1/4 cup vegan cream cheese substitute (such as Tofutti ®)
- 1/4 cup vegan margarine (such as Earth Balance®)
- 2 tablespoons vegan sour cream (such as Tofutti®)
- 2 tablespoons nutritional yeast
- 1 dash garlic powder, or to taste
- 1 dash ground nutmeg, or to taste

Direction

- Blend mozzarella-style vegan cheese, soy milk, cream cheese substitute, vegan margarine, vegan sour cream, nutritional yeast, garlic powder, and ground nutmeg in a blender until smooth.

Nutrition Information

- Calories: 527 calories
- Total Fat: 45 g
- Cholesterol: 0 mg
- Sodium: 1106 mg
- Total Carbohydrate: 15 g
- Protein: 11.1 g

Delicious & Creamy Sauces

Almond Sauce Chicken Breasts

"This tasty dish is very rich in flavour."

Serving: 4 | Prep: 20 m | Cook: 40 m | Ready in: 1 h

Ingredients

- 4 skinless, boneless chicken breast halves
- salt and pepper to taste
- 1 egg
- 1/2 cup water
- 2 cups finely chopped almonds
- 1/4 cup butter
- 3 tablespoons olive oil
- 1 pound fresh mushrooms
- 1 onion, sliced into rings
- 2 cloves garlic, crushed
- 1 cup heavy cream
- 1/4 cup almond paste
- 1/2 teaspoon freshly ground nutmeg

Direction

- Pound chicken breasts to flatten; Season with salt and pepper to taste. In a small bowl, beat together egg and water to make egg wash. Place almond crumbs in a shallow dish or bowl; dip chicken in egg wash, then dredge in almonds.

- Melt butter with olive oil in a medium skillet over medium high heat. Brown coated chicken quickly, then transfer to a 9x13 inch baking dish.
- Preheat oven to 350 degrees F (175 degrees C).
- In same skillet, brown the mushrooms and onions with the garlic. Mix together and spread mixture over the chicken.
- In same skillet, combine the cream and almond paste and mix together; heat through, then stir in nutmeg. Pour sauce over chicken, mushrooms and onions.
- Bake in preheated oven for 40 minutes, or until chicken is cooked through and no longer pink inside.

Nutrition Information

- Calories: 1095 calories
- Total Fat: 88.8 g
- Cholesterol: 227 mg
- Sodium: 206 mg
- Total Carbohydrate: 33.1 g
- Protein: 52.1 g

Asparagus with OrangeCream Sauce and Cashews

"This is a delicious and unexpected take on asparagus, handed down to me by my Aunt, Anne. Creamy and flavorful, it's sure to be a hit at your next dinner!"

Serving: 8 | Prep: 10 m | Cook: 15 m | Ready in: 25 m
Ingredients

- 2 1/2 pounds fresh asparagus
- 4 tablespoons butter
- 3 tablespoons all-purpose flour
- 2 cups heavy cream
- salt to taste
- ground white pepper to taste
- 1 large orange - peeled, sectioned, and cut into large pieces
- 1/2 cup chopped cashews
- finely grated orange zest for garnish

Direction

- Place asparagus in a steamer over 1 inch of boiling water. Cover and cook until tender but still firm, about 2 to 4 minutes. Drain, and set aside.
- Melt butter in a small saucepan over low heat. Stir in flour and cook for about 2 minutes, stirring constantly. Gradually whisk in cream and cook for about 5 minutes, stirring constantly, or until lightly thickened. Season to taste with salt and white

pepper. Remove from heat, and stir in orange pieces.
- Arrange asparagus on a serving platter, and season lightly with salt. Pour cream sauce over asparagus, and sprinkle with chopped cashews and orange zest. Serve immediately.

Nutrition Information

- Calories: 356 calories
- Total Fat: 32.1 g
- Cholesterol: 97 mg
- Sodium: 282 mg
- Total Carbohydrate: 14.9 g
- Protein: 6.2 g

Basic Bechamel Sauce

"This is a quick and easy bechamel sauce."

Serving: 8 | Prep: 5 m | Cook: 35 m | Ready in: 40 m

Ingredients

- 5 tablespoons butter
- 1/4 cup all-purpose flour
- 1 quart milk
- 2 teaspoons salt
- 1/4 teaspoon freshly grated nutmeg

Direction

- Melt butter in a large saucepan over medium heat. Once melted, stir in the flour until smooth. Continue stirring as the flour cooks to a light, golden, sandy color, about 7 minutes.
- Increase heat to medium-high and slowly whisk in milk until thickened by the roux. Bring to a gentle simmer, then reduce heat to medium-low and continue simmering until the flour has softened and not longer tastes gritty, 10 to 20 minutes, then season with salt and nutmeg.

Nutrition Information

- Calories: 139 calories
- Total Fat: 9.7 g
- Cholesterol: 29 mg
- Sodium: 683 mg
- Total Carbohydrate: 8.7 g
- Protein: 4.5 g

Basil Cream Sauce

"After a mad search on the net for a recipe for this sauce I had to create my own. This can be reheated in the microwave without the usual cream sauce defects. I just love the light green color and how well it displays over tri color or regular pasta, salmon and grilled chicken. I have been putting this on everything."

Serving: 6 | Prep: 10 m | Cook: 15 m | Ready in: 25 m
Ingredients

- 2 cups fresh basil leaves
- 4 cloves garlic, minced
- 1/4 cup olive oil
- 2 ounces pine nuts
- 1/2 cup grated Parmesan cheese
- salt and pepper to taste
- 1 pint light cream

Direction

- In a food processor, combine basil and garlic. Begin processing, and pour in olive oil in a thin stream. Process for about 40 seconds, or until mixture begins to emulsify. Add pine nuts and Parmesan, then blend for 1 minute.
- Heat cream in a saucepan over low heat until simmering. Pour 1/2 of the hot cream into the processor with basil pesto, and pulse for 20 seconds to incorporate. Pour mixture back into cream, and simmer for 5 minutes, or until thickened.

Nutrition Information

- Calories: 285 calories
- Total Fat: 28.2 g
- Cholesterol: 50 mg
- Sodium: 117 mg
- Total Carbohydrate: 3.8 g
- Protein: 6.3 g

Bechamel Sauce

"A creamy classic - your standard white sauce!"

Serving: 16
Ingredients

- 4 tablespoons butter
- 2 tablespoons grated onion
- 2 tablespoons all-purpose flour
- 1 cup chicken broth
- 1 cup half-and-half
- 1/2 teaspoon salt
- 1/4 teaspoon ground white pepper
- 1 pinch dried thyme
- 1 pinch ground cayenne pepper

Direction

- MICROWAVE METHOD: In microwave oven, melt butter in a 1-quart glass measuring pitcher for about 1 minute at HIGH.
- Add grated onion and flour and mix well. Gradually add warm or room temperature chicken broth (NOT

- hot) and half-and-half to container, stirring constantly.
- Cook uncovered for 5-6 minutes at HIGH or until sauce is thickened. Do NOT boil.
- After 2 minutes, stir mixture, then stir again every 30 seconds to one minute as needed. When sauce reaches medium thickness, remove from microwave, add seasonings and stir. Mmmm!
- STOVETOP METHOD: In a small saucepan, melt butter and stir in the flour, salt and white pepper. Add cold half-and-half and COLD chicken broth all at once. Stir well. Cook, stirring frequently, at medium heat until thick. Remove from heat and stir in seasoning.

Nutrition Information

- Calories: 52 calories
- Total Fat: 4.7 g
- Cholesterol: 13 mg
- Sodium: 147 mg
- Total Carbohydrate: 1.6 g
- Protein: 0.9 g

Blender Bearnaise Sauce

"Bearnaise sauce is delicious, but can be difficult to make over a stove because it breaks (much like hollandaise). Here is a fool-proof recipe that will surely impress your dinner guests! Keeps for 1 week in the refrigerator."

Serving: 8 | Prep: 10 m | Cook: 5 m | Ready in: 15 m

Ingredients

- 2 tablespoons white wine
- 1 tablespoon cider vinegar
- 1 teaspoon dried tarragon
- 1/2 teaspoon dried minced onion
- 1/4 teaspoon ground black pepper
- 1/2 cup butter
- 3 egg yolks
- 2 tablespoons lemon juice
- 1/2 teaspoon salt
- 1 pinch cayenne pepper

Direction

- Combine wine, vinegar, tarragon, onion, and black pepper in a skillet; bring to a boil and cook until almost all the liquid is evaporated, 2 to 3 minutes.
- Place butter in a microwave-safe bowl and heat in microwave until fully melted, 30 seconds to 1 minute.
- Place tarragon mixture, egg yolks, lemon juice, salt, and cayenne pepper in a blender; pulse until combined, 5 to 10 seconds. Remove the small hole cover from lid; stream butter into egg mixture while blender is running until sauce is completely blended and smooth.

Nutrition Information

- Calories: 127 calories
- Total Fat: 13.2 g
- Cholesterol: 107 mg
- Sodium: 231 mg

- Total Carbohydrate: 0.9 g
- Protein: 1.2 g

BLT Pasta Carbonara

"The addition of summer tomatoes and spinach to this traditional dish brings things to a whole new level. The trick to the recipe is preparation, have all the ingredients ready to go as it comes together as quickly as it takes to boil the pasta."

Serving: 6 | Prep: 15 m | Cook: 20 m | Ready in: 35 m
Ingredients

- 1 tablespoon olive oil
- 1/2 pound sliced bacon, cut into 1/2-inch pieces
- 1 cup grated Parmesan cheese
- 3 eggs
- 1 egg yolk
- salt and freshly ground black pepper to taste
- 13 1/2 ounces whole wheat elbow macaroni
- 3 cloves garlic, minced
- 1 pint cherry tomatoes, halved
- 1 bunch fresh spinach, stems removed and leaves torn into bite-sized pieces

Direction

- Heat oil in a large skillet over medium heat. Add bacon; cook, stirring occasionally until crisp and fat has rendered, 5 to 7 minutes. Remove bacon using a slotted spoon and set aside. Pour bacon fat into a

small bowl and set aside, but do not wash the skillet.
- Bring a large pot of lightly salted water to a boil.
- Mix Parmesan cheese, eggs, egg yolk, and 1/8 teaspoon black pepper together in a bowl.
- Cook elbow macaroni in the boiling water, stirring occasionally, until tender yet firm to the bite, about 8 minutes. Drain into a colander set over a large, heatproof bowl. Reserve 1 cup of the cooking water and pour the rest out, keeping the now-heated bowl in place.
- Return 1 teaspoon reserved bacon fat to the large skillet over medium heat. Add garlic and cook until fragrant, about 30 seconds. Cook 30 seconds more and add tomatoes. Cook, stirring occasionally, until heated through but not falling apart, about 5 minutes. Stir in spinach.
- Add cooked bacon, cooked tomato mixture, and cooked pasta to the heated bowl. Whisk 1/2 cup of the reserved cooking water into the egg mixture. Pour this over the pasta mixture in the bowl and toss for 3 minutes. Thin sauce if necessary by adding additional reserved cooking water. Season with salt and pepper. Serve immediately with additional Parmesan cheese.

Nutrition Information

- Calories: 432 calories
- Total Fat: 15.4 g
- Cholesterol: 141 mg
- Sodium: 601 mg

- Total Carbohydrate: 53.8 g
- Protein: 24.4 g

Cajun Ponchartrain Sauce

"My take on the Ponchartrain sauce served at a popular seafood restaurant chain in my town. Although I prefer Snapper, it may be ladled over any grilled, blackened, steamed, or pan fried fish. Very elegant and easy! Great idea for a romantic candlelight dinner for two."

Serving: 2 | Prep: 10 m | Cook: 5 m | Ready in: 15 m
Ingredients

- 1/4 cup butter
- 8 fresh mushrooms, sliced
- 8 medium shrimp - peeled and deveined
- 1/4 cup whipping cream
- garlic powder to taste
- black pepper to taste
- 2 teaspoons Madeira wine

Direction

- In a medium saucepan, sauté mushrooms in 1 teaspoon butter until tender. Stir in shrimp, and cook until pink. Transfer to a bowl.
- In the same saucepan, melt the remaining 2 teaspoons butter. Slowly mix in cream. Stir in the shrimp and mushroom mixture, and season to taste with garlic powder and black pepper. Simmer over

very low heat until thick. Just before serving, stir in wine.

Nutrition Information

- Calories: 355 calories
- Total Fat: 34.7 g
- Cholesterol: 138 mg
- Sodium: 214 mg
- Total Carbohydrate: 4.1 g
- Protein: 8 g

Chef Johns Penne with Vodka Sauce

"This is the incredibly easy and always popular vodka sauce. There are certain flavors in tomatoes that are only brought out if you introduce alcohol into the sauce."

Serving: 6 | Prep: 15 m | Cook: 50 m | Ready in: 1 h 10 m

Ingredients

- 4 ounces pancetta bacon, diced
- 1 small sprig fresh rosemary
- 1 tablespoon olive oil
- 1/2 cup vodka
- 1/2 cup heavy whipping cream
- freshly ground black pepper to taste
- 3 cups prepared marinara sauce
- 3/4 cup water
- 1 (14.5 ounce) package multigrain penne pasta (such as Barilla®)
- 1/2 cup freshly grated Parmesan cheese

Direction

- Cook and stir bacon and rosemary sprig with olive oil in a large, deep skillet over medium heat until bacon renders its fat but is not crisp, about 5 minutes. Pour vodka into the skillet, standing back to avoid any flare-ups. Raise heat to high and continue to cook until the vodka reduces to about 2 tablespoons.

- Pour heavy cream into skillet, stir briefly, and add black pepper; bring sauce to a boil. Reduce heat to medium; cook and stir until sauce has slightly reduced, 3 to 4 minutes. Mix marinara sauce and water into cream mixture and bring to a simmer. Lower heat and simmer sauce 20 to 25 minutes to blend flavors.
- Fill a large pot with salted water and bring to a boil. Stir in penne and return to a boil. Cook pasta, stirring occasionally, until cooked through but still chewy, about 10 minutes; drain and return to pot. Pour sauce over penne and stir to combine. Turn off heat, cover pot with a lid, and let stand 5 minutes for pasta to absorb sauce. Serve sprinkled with Parmesan cheese.

Nutrition Information

- Calories: 602 calories
- Total Fat: 25.1 g
- Cholesterol: 48 mg
- Sodium: 791 mg
- Total Carbohydrate: 68.4 g
- Protein: 15.9 g

Chef Johns White Sauce

"White sauce is one of the "mother sauces" in traditional culinary training and is used in many popular dishes."

Serving: 8 | Prep: 5 m | Cook: 17 m | Ready in: 22 m

Ingredients

- 1/2 cup butter
- 1/2 cup flour
- 1 quart milk
- 4 sprigs fresh thyme, chopped
- 1/8 teaspoon freshly grated nutmeg
- salt
- 1 pinch cayenne pepper, or more to taste

Direction

- Melt butter in a saucepan over low heat. Stir in flour and cook for about 5 minutes.
- Stir in 1 cup cold milk, about 1 minute. Stir in second cup of milk for an additional minute.
- Stir in remaining 2 cups of milk, cayenne pepper, salt, thyme, and nutmeg; bring to a simmer over low heat until sauce begins to thicken, about 10 minutes.

Nutrition Information

- Calories: 192 calories
- Total Fat: 14 g
- Cholesterol: 40 mg
- Sodium: 132 mg

- Total Carbohydrate: 11.8 g
- Protein: 5 g

Chipotle Chile and Blue Cheese Sauce

"Chipotle peppers add deep smoky flavor to this rich blue cheese and cream sauce. It's delicious spooned over a grilled steak. Try it with fresh pasta or drizzled over a gourmet burger, too!"

Serving: 6 | Prep: 10 m | Ready in: 10 m
Ingredients

- 5 ounces blue cheese, crumbled
- 3/4 cup heavy cream
- 3 tablespoons pureed chipotle peppers in adobo sauce
- 2 tablespoons chopped fresh chives

Direction

- Crumble blue cheese into a bowl, and mash with a fork. Pour in cream, and stir until smooth. Then transfer to a saucepan, and gently cook over low heat until warmed through. Remove from heat, and stir in pureed chipotle peppers and chives.

Nutrition Information

- Calories: 190 calories
- Total Fat: 17.9 g
- Cholesterol: 58 mg
- Sodium: 376 mg
- Total Carbohydrate: 1.9 g
- Protein: 5.7 g

Crab Cake Sauce

"A delicious creamy sauce for your crab cakes that's a breeze to make and tastes great."

Serving: 12 | Prep: 5 m | Ready in: 1 h 5 m

Ingredients

- 1 cup sour cream
- 1 cup mayonnaise
- 1/2 cup cottage cheese
- 1/3 cup hot salsa
- 1/4 teaspoon cayenne pepper
- 1 tablespoon lemon juice
- 1/2 cup plain yogurt

Direction

- Combine the sour cream, mayonnaise, cottage cheese, salsa, cayenne pepper, lemon juice and yogurt in a blender and puree until smooth. Chill before serving.

Nutrition Information

- Calories: 191 calories
- Total Fat: 19.2 g
- Cholesterol: 17 mg
- Sodium: 203 mg
- Total Carbohydrate: 2.9 g
- Protein: 2.6 g

Creamy Alfredo Sauce

"This is a great quick and easy recipe that your family will love! You may add more Parmesan, garlic, and salt to taste. You can easily add anything you like (i.e.

grilled shrimp, chicken, etc.). I also love pouring this sauce over pasta with sauteed peppers."

Serving: 4 | Prep: 10 m | Cook: 20 m | Ready in: 30 m

Ingredients

- 1/4 cup butter, or more to taste
- 1 clove garlic, minced
- 1/4 cup all-purpose flour
- 2 tablespoons grated Parmesan cheese (such as Kraft®)
- 2 cups milk
- 1 1/2 teaspoons Italian seasoning
- 1 teaspoon salt, or to taste
- 1 pinch ground black pepper

Direction

- Melt butter in a large saucepan over medium-high heat; sauté garlic until golden, 2 to 3 minutes. Lower heat to medium and gradually stir flour into garlic-butter mixture until dissolved and smooth, 3 to 5 minutes.
- Gradually stir Parmesan cheese into garlic-flour mixture until cheese is melted and mixture is thickened, 2 to 3 minutes. Slowly pour milk into cheese mixture, stirring constantly, until smooth, about 5 minutes; season with Italian seasoning, salt, and pepper. Cook and stir until sauce reaches desired consistency, 5 to 10 minutes.

Nutrition Information

- Calories: 205 calories

- Total Fat: 14.8 g
- Cholesterol: 42 mg
- Sodium: 752 mg
- Total Carbohydrate: 12.6 g
- Protein: 6.1 g

Creamy Pumpkin Sauce

"This sauce is great over pumpkin or cheese ravioli!"

Serving: 8 | Prep: 10 m | Cook: 20 m | Ready in: 30 m
Ingredients

- 2 teaspoons oil
- 1 shallot, chopped
- 2 tablespoons butter
- 2 tablespoons all-purpose flour
- 1 cup light cream
- 1 pinch salt
- 1 pinch ground cinnamon
- 1 cup pumpkin puree
- 1 cup chicken broth, or more as needed
- 1 tablespoon finely chopped fresh sage
- 1 1/2 teaspoons chopped fresh thyme

Direction

- Heat oil in a skillet over medium heat; cook and stir shallots until soft, about 10 minutes. Add butter and allow to melt. Whisk flour into butter mixture until incorporated. Stir cream, salt, and cinnamon into butter mixture and continue whisking until incorporated, about 2 minutes.

- Mix pumpkin and 1/2 cup chicken broth into cream mixture, adding more broth, 1/4 cup at a time, until desired consistency is reached. Simmer sauce until desired consistency is reached, 5 to 10 minutes. Stir sage and thyme into sauce.

Nutrition Information

- Calories: 119 calories
- Total Fat: 10 g
- Cholesterol: 28 mg
- Sodium: 246 mg
- Total Carbohydrate: 6.4 g
- Protein: 1.7 g

Easy Vodka Sauce

"This is a great and simple sauce to make. Tastes delicious over any pasta! I especially love it with lobster ravioli."

Serving: 10 | Prep: 20 m | Cook: 1 h | Ready in: 1 h 20 m

Ingredients

- 1/2 cup butter
- 1 onion, diced
- 1 cup vodka
- 2 (28 ounce) cans crushed tomatoes
- 1 pint heavy cream

Direction

- In a skillet over medium heat, sauté onion in butter until slightly brown and soft. Pour in vodka and let cook for 10 minutes. Mix in crushed tomatoes and cook for 30 minutes. Pour in heavy cream and cook for another 30 minutes.
- Watch Now

Nutrition Information

- Calories: 355 calories
- Total Fat: 27.3 g
- Cholesterol: 90 mg
- Sodium: 291 mg
- Total Carbohydrate: 13.9 g
- Protein: 3.8 g

Eggplant Fillets with Cream Sauce

"An invigorating, Asian influenced dish. Serve eggplant on a bed of Asian green bean vermicelli, or rice, and top with sauce. Excellently complimented by a chilled, dry white wine. This is a recipe I created recently. It is a work in progress, so I would welcome feedback."

Serving: 4 | Prep: 5 m | Cook: 20 m | Ready in: 1 h 25 m

Ingredients

- 2 eggplants, quartered and cut into 1/2 inch strips
- 1/2 cup soy sauce
- 1 cup unsweetened coconut cream
- 2 cups seasoned tomato sauce
- 1 tablespoon miso paste
- 1 tablespoon lime juice
- 1 1/2 tablespoons vegetable oil
- 1 dash sesame oil

Direction

- Peel some, but not all, skin from eggplant. Place eggplant in a shallow dish and cover with soy sauce. Allow to marinate for 1 hour, turning eggplant occasionally.
- In a medium saucepan, mix together coconut cream, tomato sauce, miso paste, and lime juice. Place over low heat and allow to simmer, stirring occasionally. When sauce comes to a boil, remove from heat and cover with lid.

- Heat vegetable oil and sesame oil in a wok over high heat. Fry eggplant filets a few at a time, until golden brown on both sides. You may need to replenish oil between batches. Serve eggplant over rice or noodles, with sauce spooned over top.

Nutrition Information

- Calories: 392 calories
- Total Fat: 28 g
- Cholesterol: 0 mg
- Sodium: 2658 mg
- Total Carbohydrate: 34.7 g
- Protein: 8.5 g

Four Cheese Sauce

"This four cheese sauce is great with gnocchi, fettuccini, or your choice of pasta. Garlicky French bread would be a tasty accompaniment."

Serving: 16

Ingredients

- 2 cups heavy whipping cream
- 1/2 cup butter
- 1/2 cup grated Parmesan cheese
- 1/2 cup shredded mozzarella cheese
- 1/2 cup shredded provolone cheese
- 1/2 cup grated Romano cheese

Direction

- In a medium saucepan combine whipping cream and butter. Bring to a simmer over medium heat, stirring frequently until butter melts. Gradually stir in grated Parmesan cheese, grated mozzarella cheese, grated provolone cheese, and grated Romano cheese. Reduce heat to low, and continue to stir just until all cheese is melted.
- Serve immediately, sauce will thicken upon standing.

Nutrition Information

- Calories: 204 calories
- Total Fat: 20.4 g
- Cholesterol: 68 mg
- Sodium: 193 mg
- Total Carbohydrate: 1.2 g
- Protein: 4.6 g

Fresh Fig and Prosciutto Pasta Sauce

"A yummy recipe to impress in a hurry. If you plan to eat it all yourself cut down on the figs or you'll pay later. Spoon sauce over warm plates of linguine or the like and top each the prosciutto and figs. The brie and pear alternative is great for the fall."

Serving: 4 | Prep: 10 m | Cook: 10 m | Ready in: 20 m

Ingredients

- 2 tablespoons butter
- 2 tablespoons all-purpose flour
- 1/2 teaspoon salt

- 1 cup milk
- 6 thin slices prosciutto, cut into thin strips
- 6 fresh figs, stemmed and quartered
- 1 tablespoon lemon zest
- 1/4 teaspoon lemon pepper seasoning, or to taste (optional)

Direction

- Heat butter in a saucepan over low heat; gradually stir flour into melted butter until smooth and bubbly, 2 to 4 minutes. Add salt; stir to combine. Remove from heat; gradually stir in milk until smooth.
- Return white sauce to stovetop; bring to a boil. Reduce heat and simmer over low heat.
- Cook and stir prosciutto and figs in a non-stick pan over medium heat until warm, about 5 minutes. Stir lemon zest and lemon pepper seasoning into the white sauce. Serve figs and prosciutto atop sauce.

Nutrition Information

- Calories: 191 calories
- Total Fat: 10.6 g
- Cholesterol: 29 mg
- Sodium: 592 mg
- Total Carbohydrate: 20.5 g
- Protein: 5.1 g

Garlic Sauce with Broccoli and Bacon

"Put this over your favorite pasta and top with Parmesan cheese. Even my kids will eat this!"

Serving: 6 | Prep: 10 m | Cook: 22 m | Ready in: 32 m

Ingredients

- 3 slices bacon
- 2 tablespoons minced fresh garlic
- 1 quart whole milk
- 1 (12 ounce) bag broccoli florets
- 2 teaspoons garlic powder
- salt and ground black pepper to taste
- 1/4 cup water
- 3 tablespoons all-purpose flour

Direction

- Place bacon in a large skillet and cook over medium-high heat, turning occasionally, until evenly browned, about 10 minutes. Reserve fat; drain bacon slices on paper towels.
- Place garlic in the same skillet; cook over medium heat until golden, about 2 minutes. Add milk, broccoli, garlic powder, salt, and pepper; reduce heat to medium-low. Cook and stir until milk is heated through, 5 to 7 minutes.
- Stir water and flour into the milk mixture. Cook, stirring constantly, until sauce is thickened, 5 to 7 minutes. Mix in the cooked bacon.

Nutrition Information

- Calories: 163 calories
- Total Fat: 7.4 g

- Cholesterol: 21 mg
- Sodium: 215 mg
- Total Carbohydrate: 15.8 g
- Protein: 9.2 g

GarlicTarragon Cream Sauce

"A creamy all purpose pasta sauce that will please all garlic lovers! PS: Not for the calorie counters."

Serving: 4 | Prep: 10 m | Cook: 20 m | Ready in: 30 m
Ingredients

- 1/2 cup margarine
- 4 cloves garlic, crushed
- 1/4 cup minced onion
- 1 tablespoon dried tarragon
- 1/2 cup dry white wine
- 3 cups half and half
- 1 cup grated Parmesan cheese
- 1/4 cup all-purpose flour
- 1/2 cup cold water
- salt and pepper to taste

Direction

- Melt the margarine in a large saucepan over medium-low heat. Stir in the garlic, onion, and tarragon; cook until the onion has softened, about 5 minutes. Add white wine, and cook for 5 minutes. Pour in half and half and Parmesan cheese; increase heat to medium-high and bring to a simmer.

- Whisk the flour into the water, dissolving any lumps. When the sauce has come to a boil, stir in the flour mixture to thicken to desired consistency. Season to taste with salt and pepper.

Nutrition Information

- Calories: 590 calories
- Total Fat: 49.2 g
- Cholesterol: 85 mg
- Sodium: 792 mg
- Total Carbohydrate: 18.2 g
- Protein: 14.7 g

Gorgonzola Sauce

"Extremely easy and quick pasta sauce recipe. Use for cooked chicken or shrimp, too. For a lower fat version, substitute half and half for the cream and add a teaspoon of cornstarch for thickening."

Serving: 4 | Cook: 20 m | Ready in: 20 m

Ingredients

- 1 1/2 cups dry white wine
- 1 1/4 cups heavy cream
- 2 tablespoons grated Parmesan cheese
- 4 ounces Gorgonzola cheese, crumbled
- 1 pinch ground nutmeg
- black pepper to taste

Direction

- In medium saucepan, cook white wine over high heat until reduced by half. Add cream, reduce heat, and cook until reduced by one-third. Add parmesan, gorgonzola and nutmeg. Stir until cheeses melt and sauce is creamy.

Nutrition Information

- Calories: 446 calories
- Total Fat: 36.3 g
- Cholesterol: 134 mg
- Sodium: 351 mg
- Total Carbohydrate: 4.8 g
- Protein: 8.6 g

Lobster Sauce for Mashed Potatoes

"This dish whips boring mashed potatoes into a seafood frenzy with the flavor of lobster. Great with salmon and asparagus!"

Serving: 6 | Prep: 30 m | Cook: 30 m | Ready in: 1 h

Ingredients

- 1/2 cup butter
- 2 (7 ounce) cans lobster meat, diced
- 1 medium onion, diced
- 2 large stalks celery, diced
- 2 carrots, peeled and chopped
- 1 teaspoon minced fresh thyme
- 1/8 teaspoon chopped fresh parsley
- 1 teaspoon whole black peppercorns
- 1/8 teaspoon seasoned salt

- 1 bay leaf
- 1/8 teaspoon lemon juice
- 1/4 cup all-purpose flour
- 2 tablespoons tomato paste
- 1/2 cup cream sherry
- 1 quart heavy cream
- 1/2 teaspoon salt and pepper to taste

Direction

- Melt the butter in a large pot over medium heat. Stir in the lobster, onion, celery, carrot, thyme, parsley, peppercorns, seasoned salt, bay leaf, and lemon juice. Cook, stirring constantly, over medium heat to soften the vegetables, about 10 minutes. Stir in the flour and tomato paste; cook for another 5 minutes, stirring constantly. Pour in sherry and cook for a minute or two to cook off the alcohol.
- Pour in the heavy cream, and bring to a simmer. Reduce heat to low, simmer until the sauce has thickened, and will coat the back of a spoon, about 15 minutes. Strain through a fine mesh strainer, and discard the solids. Season to taste with salt and pepper.

Nutrition Information

- Calories: 804 calories
- Total Fat: 74.8 g
- Cholesterol: 320 mg
- Sodium: 770 mg
- Total Carbohydrate: 17.4 g
- Protein: 17 g

Mango Cream Sauce

"I was making Anniversary Chicken, and wondered what I could put on the plate with it... Pasta didn't work, so I re-created this sauce that a chef in a restaurant told me about once. Leave out the mango slices if they will clash with the type of chicken you are cooking."

Serving: 6 | Prep: 10 m | Cook: 15 m | Ready in: 25 m

Ingredients

- 1 cup heavy cream
- 1 (15.25 ounce) can mango slices, with juice
- 1 (1.5 fluid ounce) jigger brandy
- 2 tablespoons brown sugar

Direction

- In a medium saucepan over medium heat, blend heavy cream, mango juice, brandy, and brown sugar until thickened. Stir in mangoes, and bring to a boil over high heat. Continue to cook and stir about 1 minute. Serve warm.

Nutrition Information

- Calories: 206 calories
- Total Fat: 14.8 g
- Cholesterol: 54 mg
- Sodium: 23 mg
- Total Carbohydrate: 13.9 g
- Protein: 0.9 g

Mushroom Cream Sauce With Shallots

"This is one of my favorite sauce recipes. It is the best cream sauce you will ever have."

Serving: 3 | Prep: 10 m | Cook: 15 m | Ready in: 25 m

Ingredients

- 2 lobster mushrooms, cut into cubes
- 2 tablespoons water
- 1/3 cup heavy whipping cream
- 2 teaspoons all-purpose flour
- 2 tablespoons grated Asiago cheese
- 1/2 shallot, minced
- 1/2 teaspoon salt
- 1/2 teaspoon ground black pepper

Direction

- Place mushrooms in a nonstick skillet over medium heat; add water. Cook, stirring occasionally, until water is evaporated, about 5 minutes.
- Whisk cream and flour into mushrooms until flour is incorporated. Add Asiago cheese, shallot, salt, and black pepper to mushroom mixture, stirring constantly. Cook and stir until sauce thickens, about 7 minutes.

Nutrition Information

- Calories: 123 calories
- Total Fat: 11.1 g
- Cholesterol: 40 mg
- Sodium: 454 mg

- Total Carbohydrate: 4.1 g
- Protein: 2.5 g

Mussels in Curry Cream Sauce

"Mussels steamed in a curry cream sauce, an easy and delicious recipe, you'll love it!"

Serving: 4 | Prep: 40 m | Cook: 15 m | Ready in: 55 m
Ingredients

- 1/2 cup minced shallots
- 2 tablespoons minced garlic
- 1 1/2 cups dry white wine
- 1 cup heavy cream
- 1 teaspoon curry powder
- 32 mussels - cleaned and debearded
- 1/4 cup butter
- 1/4 cup minced parsley
- 1/4 cup chopped green onions

Direction

- In a large saucepan, cook shallots and garlic in simmering wine until translucent.
- Stir in cream and curry powder. When sauce is heated through, add mussels. Cover, and steam mussels for a few minutes, until their shells open wide. With a slotted spoon, transfer steamed mussels to a bowl, leaving the sauce in the pan. Discard any unopened mussels.

- Whisk butter into the cream sauce. Turn heat off, and stir in parsley and green onions. Serve immediately.

Nutrition Information

- Calories: 446 calories
- Total Fat: 35.5 g
- Cholesterol: 128 mg
- Sodium: 172 mg
- Total Carbohydrate: 10.7 g
- Protein: 6.4 g

Nicks Pepper Sauce Sauce au Poivre

"A very easy and tasty black pepper sauce that goes with a steak."

Serving: 6 | Prep: 10 m | Cook: 20 m | Ready in: 30 m

Ingredients

- 2 tablespoons butter
- 1/4 cup finely minced shallots
- 6 tablespoons finely chopped fresh parsley
- 1 tablespoon crushed black pepper
- 1/2 teaspoon salt
- 1 cup cognac
- 1 1/2 cups beef stock
- 6 tablespoons creme fraiche
- 2 tablespoons butter

Direction

- Melt 2 tablespoons butter in a saucepan over low heat. Cook and stir shallots in hot butter until

translucent, about 5 minutes. Add parsley and sauté for 5 minutes; season with pepper and salt.
- Carefully pour cognac over shallot mixture; cook and stir until flames have disappeared, 2 to 3 minutes. Add beef stock and bring to a boil; reduce heat, add creme fraiche, and simmer until sauce is slightly reduced, about 5 minutes. Stir 2 tablespoons butter into sauce until melted.

Nutrition Information

- Calories: 249 calories
- Total Fat: 13.6 g
- Cholesterol: 41 mg
- Sodium: 279 mg
- Total Carbohydrate: 3.4 g
- Protein: 2 g

NoCook Cashew Alfredo

"This is an amazing recipe when it's the middle of summer and you don't feel like working in the kitchen. Light and refreshing, yet quick and easy! Serve over zucchini noodles or regular noodles."

Serving: 6 | Prep: 10 m | Ready in: 10 m

Ingredients

- 2 cups cashews
- 1 1/2 cups water
- 1/2 cup pine nuts
- 1/4 cup nutritional yeast
- 3 cloves garlic

- 1 tablespoon lemon juice
- 1 teaspoon sea salt
- 1 teaspoon dried thyme
- ground black pepper to taste

Direction

- Blend cashews, water, pine nuts, nutritional yeast, garlic, lemon juice, sea salt, thyme, and pepper together in a blender or food processor until smooth.

Nutrition Information

- Calories: 347 calories
- Total Fat: 27.2 g
- Cholesterol: 0 mg
- Sodium: 590 mg
- Total Carbohydrate: 19.2 g
- Protein: 12.5 g

Pink Sauce for Pasta Shrimp

"Great with pasta or rice."

Serving: 4 | Prep: 5 m | Cook: 10 m | Ready in: 15 m

Ingredients

- 4 tablespoons tomato puree
- 3/4 cup water
- 1 cup heavy cream
- 1 1/2 teaspoons grated fresh ginger root
- 1/4 teaspoon cayenne pepper

- 4 teaspoons lemon juice
- 1 teaspoon ground cumin
- 1 teaspoon salt
- ground black pepper to taste
- 1/2 teaspoon white sugar
- 3 tablespoons vegetable oil
- 1 tablespoon mustard seed
- 2 cloves garlic, chopped
- 2 pounds medium shrimp - peeled and deveined
- salt to taste
- ground black pepper to taste

Direction

- Place tomato puree in a measuring cup. Add enough water to make a total measure of 1 cup, place in a medium bowl. Stir in cream, ginger, cayenne pepper, lemon juice, cumin, 1 teaspoon salt, black pepper to taste, and sugar. Cover and refrigerate until needed.
- Heat oil in a large frying pan over a medium-high heat. Add the mustard seeds. As soon as they begin to pop, add the garlic. Stir once and add the shrimps. Stir and fry until they just turn opaque, sprinkling with salt and pepper to taste.
- Pour in the pink sauce and stir. As soon as the sauce is bubbling, the dish is ready to be served with hot cooked pasta or rice.

Nutrition Information

- Calories: 565 calories
- Total Fat: 37.2 g

- Cholesterol: 427 mg
- Sodium: 1004 mg
- Total Carbohydrate: 8 g
- Protein: 48.5 g

Pressure Cooker Creamy Cauliflower Cheese Sauce

"A healthy alternative to Alfredo or white sauce. Freezes beautifully and can be used on pasta, potatoes, other veggies, or on pizza. You won't believe how good this is - even my very picky son loved it! Can be made Paleo, vegetarian, or dairy free. Use immediately or freeze for up to 6 months."

Serving: 4 | Prep: 30 m | Cook: 8 m | Ready in: 38 m
Ingredients

- 2 teaspoons butter
- 5 cloves garlic, minced
- 1 head cauliflower, florets separated and stems cut into 1/2-inch pieces
- 1 cup low-sodium chicken stock
- 1/2 cup water (optional)
- 1/2 cup grated Parmesan cheese (optional)
- salt and ground black pepper to taste

Direction

- Melt butter in an electric pressure cooker on the "Sauté" setting. Add garlic; cook and stir until fragrant, about 2 minutes. Add cauliflower and

chicken stock. Seal cooker and bring to high pressure according to manufacturer's directions. Cook for 6 minutes.
- Release pressure naturally according to manufacturer's instructions. Remove the lid carefully. Blend cauliflower with an immersion blender until creamy. Thin with water to desired consistency; stir in Parmesan cheese. Season with salt and pepper.

Nutrition Information

- Calories: 108 calories
- Total Fat: 5.2 g
- Cholesterol: 15 mg
- Sodium: 279 mg
- Total Carbohydrate: 9.5 g
- Protein: 7.8 g

Pumpkin Ravioli with Creamy Crab Sauce

"In grocery stores across the country, frozen and fresh pumpkin raviolis are popping up and selling like hot cakes. The only question is: What kind of sauce do you put on them? I've got a creamy and light crab sauce with a touch of Parmesan and thyme that will blow your mind! Sprinkle with extra cheese, garnish with a sprig of fresh thyme, and enjoy!"

Serving: 4 | Prep: 5 m | Cook: 19 m | Ready in: 24 m

Ingredients

- 1 pound frozen pumpkin-filled ravioli
- 2 tablespoons butter
- 1 (6 ounce) can crabmeat
- 2 teaspoons crushed dried thyme
- 1 pint light cream
- 1/4 cup shredded Parmesan cheese
- salt and ground white pepper to taste

Direction

- Bring a large pot of lightly salted water to a boil. Stir in ravioli and return to a boil. Cook uncovered, stirring occasionally, until ravioli float to the top and filling is hot, 6 to 8 minutes. Drain.
- Melt butter in a large saucepan over medium heat. Add crabmeat and thyme; cook and stir until thyme is fragrant, about 2 minutes. Pour in cream. Increase heat to medium-high and cook, stirring, until cream begins to steam, 4 to 5 minutes. Reduce heat and add Parmesan cheese; stir until melted, about 2 minutes.
- Ladle cream sauce into the bottom of a serving dish; top with ravioli.

Nutrition Information

- Calories: 3566 calories
- Total Fat: 57.2 g
- Cholesterol: 543 mg
- Sodium: 2086 mg
- Total Carbohydrate: 578.2 g
- Protein: 175.8 g

Roasted Garlic Peppercorn Sauce

"A rich roasted garlic white sauce made with a blend of peppercorns to give it a more exotic flavor. Toss with favorite cooked pasta and grated cheese (Asiago is great!)."

Serving: 4 | Prep: 10 m | Cook: 55 m | Ready in: 1 h 5 m

Ingredients

- 1 whole head garlic
- 1 teaspoon olive oil
- 2 tablespoons butter
- 1 1/2 tablespoons all-purpose flour
- 1 1/2 cups milk
- 1/2 teaspoon salt
- 1 tablespoon ground mixed peppercorns
- 1 pinch ground nutmeg

Direction

- Preheat the oven to 325 degrees F (165 degrees C). Slice off the top third of the head of garlic so the tips of the cloves are exposed. Place in a small baking dish, and add just enough water to cover the bottom of the dish. Drizzle the olive oil over the top of the garlic, then cover with a lid or foil. Bake for 45 minutes.
- Melt butter in a saucepan over medium heat. Mix together the flour and milk so there are no lumps, and pour into the pan with the butter. Bring to a

boil, and cook, stirring constantly until thickened, about 5 minutes. Squeeze the garlic cloves from their skin, and mash. Stir garlic into the sauce, and season with salt, peppercorns, and nutmeg.

Nutrition Information

- Calories: 144 calories
- Total Fat: 9 g
- Cholesterol: 23 mg
- Sodium: 372 mg
- Total Carbohydrate: 12.3 g
- Protein: 4.5 g

Roasted Red Pepper Cream Sauce

"A light and creamy sauce with puree of roasted red peppers as the base. It is excellent on any type of pasta, but tortellini or ravioli seems to be the best match. The prep time is rather long, but the result is definitely worth it. Freezes well. In fact, the taste may improve slightly."

Serving: 8 | Prep: 30 m | Cook: 20 m | Ready in: 50 m

Ingredients

- 2 large red bell peppers
- 2 tablespoons minced garlic
- 1/4 cup fresh basil
- 3 tablespoons extra virgin olive oil
- 2 cups half-and-half
- 1/4 cup grated Romano cheese
- 4 tablespoons butter

- salt and pepper to taste

Direction

- Preheat broiler. Lightly coat the red peppers with olive oil. Grill peppers under the broiler until the skin is blackened, and the flesh has softened slightly. Place peppers in a paper bag or resealable plastic bag to cool for approximately 45 minutes.
- Remove the seeds and skin from the peppers (the skin should come off the peppers easily now). Cut peppers into small pieces.
- In a skillet, cook and stir the garlic, basil, and red peppers in 3 tablespoons olive oil over medium heat. Cook for 10 minutes, so that the flavors mix.
- Place mixture in blender (careful it is hot), and puree to desired consistency. Return puree to skillet, and reheat to a boil. Stir in the half-and-half and the Romano cheese; cook and stir until the cheese melts. Add the butter, and stir until melted. Season with salt and pepper to taste. Simmer for 5 minutes.

Nutrition Information

- Calories: 206 calories
- Total Fat: 18.9 g
- Cholesterol: 42 mg
- Sodium: 258 mg
- Total Carbohydrate: 5.9 g
- Protein: 3.6 g

Seafood Wine Sauc

"Sauce is to be used on grilled fish or blackened fish."

Serving: 6 | Prep: 15 m | Cook: 30 m | Ready in: 45 m

Ingredients

- 1/2 cup butter
- 1/2 cup all-purpose flour
- 1 teaspoon dried basil
- 1/2 teaspoon dried thyme
- 1 tablespoon cooking oil
- 1/2 cup diced shallots
- 1 cup white wine
- 1 cup heavy cream
- 4 tablespoons butter
- salt and pepper to taste

Direction

- To make roux: Melt 1/2 cup butter in a skillet over medium heat. Stir in flour, reduce heat to low, and cook until roux is a light chocolate color. Season with basil and thyme. Remove from heat.
- Heat oil in a saucepan over medium heat. Sauté shallots until tender. Stir in wine, and simmer until liquid is reduced by half. Strain shallots from wine, and return wine to skillet. Stir in cream and 4 tablespoons butter; heat until butter is melted. Stir in 2 to 3 tablespoons of the roux, until mixture thickens. Cook on low heat for about 5 minutes to eliminate starchy flavor. Season with salt and pepper.

Nutrition Information

- Calories: 443 calories
- Total Fat: 40.1 g
- Cholesterol: 115 mg
- Sodium: 231 mg
- Total Carbohydrate: 12.5 g
- Protein: 2.5 g

Simple Lobster Scampi

"An easy way to use pre-cooked lobster. Simple, fast, and delicious! You can substitute shrimp or scallops for the lobster. This recipe is really suited to your tastes, that is why so many of the measurements are approximate. I have made this often and never measure anything, and it comes out delicious every time! Serve over your choice of cooked pasta. T"

Serving: 6 | Prep: 15 m | Cook: 27 m | Ready in: 42 m
Ingredients

- 3/4 cup butter
- 1 1/2 tablespoons minced garlic, or to taste
- 1 1/2 pounds cooked lobster meat, cut into bite-size pieces
- 1/2 cup white wine, or to taste
- 1 teaspoon lemon juice
- 1/4 cup grated Parmesan cheese, or to taste
- 1/2 cup bread crumbs, or more as needed

Direction

- Melt butter in a skillet over medium heat. Add garlic; cook and stir until aromatic, about 5 minutes.

Add lobster and cook until heated through, 5 to 10 minutes. Add wine and lemon juice; bring to a boil. Add Parmesan cheese; cook until melted, about 2 minutes. Add bread crumbs slowly, 2 tablespoons at a time, bringing to a boil after each addition.

Nutrition Information

- Calories: 385 calories
- Total Fat: 25.1 g
- Cholesterol: 146 mg
- Sodium: 713 mg
- Total Carbohydrate: 9.4 g
- Protein: 26.1 g

Smoked Salmon Vodka Cream Sauce

"A rich and creamy sauce that will complement your favorite pasta. Easy to double or triple if you need more than two servings' worth. Serve with your favorite pasta."

Serving: 2

Ingredients

- 1 tablespoon butter
- 1 tablespoon finely diced onion
- 1/2 cup diced smoked salmon
- 2 fluid ounces vodka
- 1/4 cup heavy whipping cream
- 1/4 cup chopped tomatoes
- 1/2 cup tomato sauce
- salt to taste

- ground black pepper to taste
- 1 pinch ground nutmeg
- 1/8 tablespoon cayenne pepper

Direction

- In a large saucepan sauté butter and onion with smoked salmon. Once the pan begins to lightly smoke, pull saucepan away from heat source and add the Vodka.
- When the Vodka has burned off, return the sauce to heat source and mix in the tomatoes, tomato sauce and heavy cream.
- Season sauce with salt, pepper, nutmeg, and chile pepper. Reduce sauce to desired consistency; serve.

Nutrition Information

- Calories: 282 calories
- Total Fat: 18.6 g
- Cholesterol: 64 mg
- Sodium: 641 mg
- Total Carbohydrate: 5.9 g
- Protein: 8 g

Spicy Shrimp in Cream Sauce

"Shrimp in a spicy cream sauce to be served as an appetizer with hot-baked French bread (for dipping), or over fettuccini (as a not-so-light meal). Fun to prepare in front of guests as a prelude to a nice seafood dinner! Use any hot pepper you like, Cajun seasoning, or even hotter!"

Serving: 4 | Prep: 10 m | Cook: 10 m | Ready in: 20 m

Ingredients

- 1 tablespoon extra-virgin olive oil
- 2 habanero peppers, seeded and chopped
- 1 tablespoon hot chili powder
- 4 cloves garlic, crushed
- 1 pound medium shrimp - peeled and deveined
- 1 pint heavy cream
- salt and white pepper to taste (optional)
- 1 French baguette, sliced

Direction

- Heat olive oil in a large skillet over medium-low heat. Add habanero peppers, and garlic, and fry for a few minutes to release the flavors. Add shrimp, and cook stirring constantly until pink, about 5 minutes. Season with chili powder, salt and pepper, stirring to evenly coat the shrimp. Stir in the cream, and cook over low heat until heated through, but do not allow to boil. Serve hot with bread slices.

Nutrition Information

- Calories: 868 calories
- Total Fat: 50.8 g
- Cholesterol: 336 mg
- Sodium: 1002 mg
- Total Carbohydrate: 69.7 g
- Protein: 34.8 g

TomatoCream Sauce for Pasta

"Serve over your favorite pasta. Absolutely delicious and so easy to make!"

Serving: 5 | Prep: 5 m | Cook: 15 m | Ready in: 20 m

Ingredients

- 2 tablespoons olive oil
- 1 onion, diced
- 1 clove garlic, minced
- 1 (14.5 ounce) can Italian-style diced tomatoes, undrained
- 1 tablespoon dried basil leaves
- 3/4 teaspoon white sugar
- 1/4 teaspoon dried oregano
- 1/4 teaspoon salt
- 1/8 teaspoon ground black pepper
- 1/2 cup heavy cream
- 1 tablespoon butter

Direction

- In a saucepan, sauté onion and garlic in olive oil over medium heat. Make sure it doesn't burn. Add tomatoes, basil, sugar, oregano, salt and pepper. Bring to boil and continue to boil 5 minutes or until most of the liquid evaporates. Remove from heat; stir in whipping cream and butter. Reduce heat and simmer 5 more minutes.

Nutrition Information

- Calories: 182 calories
- Total Fat: 16.6 g
- Cholesterol: 39 mg

- Sodium: 270 mg
- Total Carbohydrate: 6.7 g
- Protein: 1.7 g

Vodka Sauce

"This is a great recipe for those who love spicy food. If not, simply omit the crushed red pepper. This recipe will have your family eating the leftovers out of the refrigerator. A piece of advice: use the best vodka you can - it really makes a big difference! Serve with pasta, and garnish with grated Parmesan cheese."

Serving: 4 | Prep: 15 m | Cook: 30 m | Ready in: 45 m
Ingredients

- 1 cup vodka
- 1 teaspoon crushed red pepper flakes
- 2 tablespoons olive oil
- 3/4 pound prosciutto, chopped
- 1 large clove garlic, minced
- 2 tablespoons chopped fresh parsley
- 2 tablespoons chopped fresh basil
- salt and pepper to taste
- 1 (28 ounce) can roma tomatoes, with juice
- 2 (8 ounce) cans tomato sauce
- 1 cup heavy cream

Direction

- In a small bowl, combine vodka and red pepper flakes. Set aside for 1 hour.

- Heat olive oil in a large skillet over medium heat. Sauté prosciutto, garlic, parsley, basil, salt and pepper until prosciutto is evenly brown. Pour in vodka mixture, and simmer 10 minutes. Crush tomatoes, and stir in with 2 cans of tomato sauce, and 1 (8 ounce) can water. Simmer 15 minutes. Stir in 1 cup heavy cream, and cook 2 minutes.

Nutrition Information
- Calories: 781 calories
- Total Fat: 56.3 g
- Cholesterol: 156 mg
- Sodium: 3119 mg
- Total Carbohydrate: 16.5 g
- Protein: 21 g

White Cheese Sauce

"This is an awesome Monterey Jack sauce that goes great over chicken enchiladas, or used as a dip for chips or Mexican-style appetizers."

Serving: 20 | Prep: 10 m | Cook: 20 m | Ready in: 30 m
Ingredients

- 1 cup butter
- 3 cups shredded Monterey Jack cheese
- 1 cup sour cream
- 2 (4 ounce) cans diced green chilies, drained

Direction

- Melt butter in a saucepan over medium heat. Reduce heat to medium-low, and stir in shredded cheese until melted. Mix in sour cream and green chilies, and cook, stirring occasionally just until heated through. Do not allow to boil.

Nutrition Information

- Calories: 172 calories
- Total Fat: 16.8 g
- Cholesterol: 45 mg
- Sodium: 294 mg
- Total Carbohydrate: 1.2 g
- Protein: 4.7 g

White Cream Sauce

"Serve as a sauce for gravy, pasta and vegetables."

Serving: 8 | Prep: 5 m | Cook: 10 m | Ready in: 15 m

Ingredients

- 2 cups heavy cream
- 1/2 cup all-purpose flour
- 1 lemon, juiced

Direction

- In a saucepan stir together cream, flour and juice from a lemon. Cook until thickened.

Nutrition Information

- Calories: 236 calories
- Total Fat: 22.1 g
- Cholesterol: 82 mg
- Sodium: 23 mg
- Total Carbohydrate: 9.1 g
- Protein: 2.2 g

White Pizza Sauce

"Great for vegetable pizza, meat pizza, or pasta. Brush your favorite pizza dough with olive oil, spread sauce, add your favorite toppings, and bake per dough instructions. Also great for calzones or chicken, or chicken and broccoli with fettucine. Makes enough sauce for 2 medium pizzas. Freezes beautifully. Just thaw at room temperature."

Serving: 2 | Prep: 10 m | Cook: 8 m | Ready in: 18 m

Ingredients

- 2 tablespoons butter
- 1 tablespoon olive oil

- 1/4 cup finely chopped onion
- 1 large clove garlic, minced
- 3 tablespoons all-purpose flour
- 1 cup milk, or more as needed
- 1/2 cup grated Parmesan cheese
- 2 tablespoons minced fresh basil
- 1/2 teaspoon chopped fresh oregano (optional)
- 1/4 teaspoon salt
- 1/8 teaspoon ground black pepper

Direction

- Heat butter and olive oil in a small saucepan over medium heat; cook and stir onion and garlic until tender and fragrant, about 1 minute. Add flour and whisk until flour is lightly browned and onion is translucent, 2 to 3 minutes.
- Mix milk, Parmesan cheese, basil, oregano, salt, and black pepper into onion mixture. Cook, whisking continuously, until cheese is melted and sauce has thickened slightly, about 5 minutes. Remove from heat.

Nutrition Information

- Calories: 365 calories
- Total Fat: 26.6 g
- Cholesterol: 58 mg
- Sodium: 730 mg
- Total Carbohydrate: 18.5 g
- Protein: 13.5 g

White Sauce for Pasta

"My husband lived in Italy for 3 years, so he's really picky about his Italian cuisine! I needed a great meal that was super-quick one night for his dinner; I had spicy battered shrimp on hand that I wanted to use and a couple choices of dried pasta. This sauce sounded perfect to tie it all together!

Served over tortiglioni pasta with salad and toasted Italian bread. Just like I spent all day on dinner. It is really hard to mess-up this kind of white sauce. In my opinion, it was very much like an Alfredo sauce! Of course there is very little difference in the two sauces."

Serving: 4 | Prep: 5 m | Cook: 10 m | Ready in: 15 m

Ingredients

- 2 tablespoons butter
- 2 tablespoons margarine
- 3 tablespoons all-purpose flour
- 1 cube chicken bouillon, crumbled
- 1 1/2 cups boiling water
- 1 cup 2% milk
- ground white pepper to taste

Direction

- Melt butter and margarine in a saucepan over medium-low heat; stir in flour and bouillon until roux is well blended. Continue to cook and stir until thickened and lightly browned, about 5 minutes. Increase heat to medium and whisk water into roux until smooth. Stir in milk; cook and stir until thickened, about 2 minutes more. Season with white pepper.

Nutrition Information

- Calories: 153 calories
- Total Fat: 12.4 g
- Cholesterol: 20 mg
- Sodium: 419 mg
- Total Carbohydrate: 7.8 g
- Protein: 2.9 g

White Sauce with Ham and Herbs

"This is an easy recipe that works well over short noodles or toast."

Serving: 4 | Prep: 10 m | Cook: 40 m | Ready in: 50 m

Ingredients

- 1 tablespoon olive oil
- 1 onion, minced
- 1 cup finely chopped ham
- 1 cup water
- 1 cube chicken bouillon
- 2 tablespoons chopped fresh parsley
- 2 tablespoons chopped fresh basil
- 1/4 teaspoon ground black pepper
- 1 cup heavy whipping cream

Direction

- Heat the olive oil in a large skillet over medium-high heat. Stir in the onion and ham; cook until onions

- turn translucent. Pour in the water; season with the boullion cube, parsley, basil, and black pepper.
- Simmer for 30 minutes, uncovered, stirring occasionally. Pour in the heavy cream, and simmer for an additional 2 minutes.

Nutrition Information

- Calories: 312 calories
- Total Fat: 28.4 g
- Cholesterol: 98 mg
- Sodium: 692 mg
- Total Carbohydrate: 8.7 g
- Protein: 6.8 g

White Wine and Mushroom Sauce

"Mushrooms, peppers, onions, and garlic combined with white wine make a simply elegant dish."

Serving: 4 | Prep: 15 m | Cook: 30 m | Ready in: 45 m

Ingredients

- 2 tablespoons unsalted butter
- 5 cloves garlic
- 1 green bell pepper, diced
- 1 small onion, chopped
- 1 (8 ounce) package sliced fresh mushrooms
- 1 cup white wine
- 1 cup chicken broth
- 2 tablespoons cornstarch
- 1/4 cup cold water
- 1/4 cup heavy cream
- 1/4 cup grated Romano cheese
- 1/4 cup grated Parmesan cheese

Direction

- Melt butter in a heavy skillet over medium heat. Cook garlic in hot butter until browned, about 5 minutes.
- Mash the garlic in the skillet and stir into the butter; add green bell pepper and onion and cook until the onion is translucent, 5 to 7 minutes.
- Stir mushrooms into the pepper and onion mixture; cook and stir until the mushrooms are slightly browned, about 5 minutes. Stream heavy cream

- into the mixture while stirring; add Romano cheese and Parmesan cheese. Continue cooking until the mixture is hot and the cheese is melted, 5 to 10 minutes more.
- Pour wine into the skillet and cook until the liquid is reduced in volume by half, 5 to 10 minutes; add chicken broth, bring to a simmer, and cook until slightly reduced, about 5 minutes.
- Mix water and cornstarch together in a small bowl until cornstarch is completely dissolved; stir into the liquid in the skillet and cook, stirring regularly, until the liquid is thickened, 5 to 10 minutes.

Nutrition Information

- Calories: 254 calories
- Total Fat: 15.1 g
- Cholesterol: 49 mg
- Sodium: 421 mg
- Total Carbohydrate: 12.5 g
- Protein: 7.4 g

Tasty Pasta Recipes

1) Farfalle with Creamy Wild Mushroom Sauce

This is a rather creamy pasta dish that is full of flavor. The mushroom used in the dish can be found in 8-ounce packages. This dish is just delectable and a must try.

Yield: 8

Cooking Time: 20 minutes

List of Ingredients:
- Farfalle (1 lb., uncooked)
- Butter (1 tablespoon)
- Mushroom (12ozs., sliced)
- Onion (½ cup, chopped)
- Shallots (⅓ cup, chopped)
- Garlic (1 tablespoon, minced)
- Salt (1 ½ teaspoons)

- Black pepper (¼ teaspoons)
- White wine (¼ cup, dry)
- Whipping cream (⅔ cup)
- Parmigiano-Reggiano cheese (½ cup, grated)
- Parsley (2 tablespoons, chopped)

Procedure:

Allow pasta to cook using the directions on the package. Drain and set aside. Melt the butter in a skillet over medium heat and add onions, garlic, mushrooms, shallots, a teaspoons pepper and a teaspoons salt. Cook until mushrooms are completely tender (should be about 12 minutes). Pour in the wine and cook for a further 2 minutes (liquid will evaporate). Gently stir and set aside. Combine the cheese, pasta, 2 tablespoons parsley and whipping cream then pour the pasta mixture into the mushroom mix you prepared previously. Gently toss until evenly coated and serve. Enjoy.

2) Shrimp Fra Diavolo

Pasta dishes using Shrimp Diavolo can sometimes be very spicy and hot but not to worry spice can be lessened or increased based on liking without losing flavor.

Yield: 4

Cooking Time:

List of Ingredients:

- Uncooked linguine (8 oz.)
- Olive oil (2 tablespoons, Extra-virgin)
- Garlic (1 ½ tablespoons diced)
- Medium shrimp (1 pound)
- Onion (¾ cup, diced)
- Red pepper (1 teaspoon, crushed)
- Basil (½ teaspoon, dried)
- Oregano (½ teaspoon, dried)
- Tomato paste (2 tablespoons)
- Lemon juice (1 tablespoon, freshly squeezed)
- Can tomatoes (1 ¾ cups, crushed)
- Salt (¼ teaspoon)
- Can tomatoes, (14.5-ounce diced, drained)

Procedure:

Cook pasta as directed on package excluding salt then drain and cover to keep warm. In a large skillet (preferably nonstick) heat a tablespoon of oil and add a half teaspoon of garlic along with shrimp. Sauté shrimps until done and remove from pan; cover to keep warm. Put a tablespoon of oil and onion in pan and sauté until soft. Put in remaining 1 tablespoon garlic, basil, pepper, and oregano and allow to cook for a minute, constantly stirring. Add in lemon juice and lemon tomato paste; cook 1 minute till it gets slightly dark. Finally add in crushed and diced tomatoes along with salt, and cook for 5 minutes till the mix gets thick. Add shrimp to the mixture and cook for 2 minutes or until it is heated thoroughly. Serve with pasta.

3) Fettuccine Alfredo with Bacon

If you love Fettuccine then this recipe will be perfect for you as it pairs your glorified fettuccine pasta with smoked bacon and Parmigiano cheese.

Yield: 4

Cooking Time: 20 minutes

List of Ingredients:
- Fettuccine (9oz., fresh)
- Bacon (2 slices, chopped)
- Garlic (1 teaspoon, diced)
- Flour (1 tablespoon, all purpose)
- Milk (1 cup)
- Parmigiano cheese (⅔ cup)

- Salt (½ teaspoon)
- Parsley (2 tablespoons., chopped)
- Black pepper (½ teaspoons)

Procedure:

Allow pasta to cook using the directions on the package. Drain the pasta and hold back 1/3 cup of the cooking liquid and set aside. Proceed to cook the bacon on a medium flame until crisp (should be about 4 minutes); reserve the bacon drippings from the pan. Mix in a bit of garlic to the drippings and allow to sauté for about a minute. Sprinkle the flour in the skillet on top of the garlic, stirring continuously, and allow cooking for about 20 seconds. Continue to stir constantly then add the milk a bit at a time, until finished; allow cooking until the mixture becomes slightly thick and is bubbling (should be about 2 minutes). Reduce to low heat and add cheese, a bit at a time, while stirring and allow cooking until the cheese is completely melted. Now prepare the reserved cooking liquid by seasoning it with a dash of salt. Pour your hot pasta in the cooking liquid and toss until combined. Top with parsley, pepper and bacon. Serve and enjoy.

4) Cavatappi with Bacon and Summer Vegetables

This is a dish that is easy to prepare and absolutely delicious dinner idea and great for those people watching their calories. A mixture of cavatappi and bacon accented with vegetables whatever you can find is fine. Healthy, low in calories and mouthwatering. What are you waiting for!

Yield: 4

Cooking Time: 20 minutes

List of Ingredients:

- Uncooked cavatappi (8oz.)
- Bacon (4 slices chopped)
- Olive oil (2 teaspoons)
- Onion (1 cup chopped)
- Garlic (1 teaspoon minced)
- Zucchini (medium, cut ¼ inch thick)
- Corn kernels (1 cup)
- Tomatoes (grape 1 pint)
- Cheese (Parmigiano-Reggiano, ½ cup shredded)
- Fresh basil leaves (small, ¼ cup)
- Salt (½ teaspoons)
- Black pepper (¼ teaspoons)

Procedure:
Firstly cook pasta as directed on package, excluding salt then drain. Over medium heat cook bacon until crisp in a large nonstick skillet .Use a slotted spoon to take bacon from skillet, leave drippings in pan. Then add oil to the drippings in pan. Put onion and garlic in pan and sauté for 2 minutes occasionally stirring. Add zucchini and cook for 3 minutes. Add in tomatoes and corn and allow to cook. Add mixture to the pasta and toss. Allow to cook for a minute or until heated thoroughly. Remove the pasta from the flame and add cheese ¼ cup), basil, ½ teaspoon salt and pepper and toss. After tossing sprinkle with cheese that's left. Serve with your favourite green salad and enjoy!

5) Baked Ziti and Summer Veggies

Seeking a healthy alternative to the regular fatty pasta. Then recipe will be the perfect fit for you.

Yield: 4

Cooking Time: 40 minutes

List of Ingredients:
- Ziti (4ozs., uncooked)
- Olive oil (1 tablespoon)
- Squash (2 cups, yellow, chopped)
- Zucchini (1 cup, chopped)
- Onion (½ cup, chopped)
- Tomato (2 cups, chopped)

- Garlic (2 cloves, minced)
- Mozzarella Cheese (1 Cup, part skimmed, shredded)
- Basil (2 tablespoons, chopped)
- Oregano (2 teaspoons chopped)
- Salt (¾ teaspoons)
- Red pepper (⅛ teaspoons, chopped)
- Ricotta Cheese (¼ cup, part - skimmed)
- Egg (1 large, lightly beaten)
- Cooking spray for coating

Procedure:

Allow pasta to cook using the directions on the package. Drain and set aside. Set your oven to preheat at 400°. Sauté squash, onions, and zucchini for 5 minutes over a medium flame. Move away from the stove and stir in pasta with ½ teaspoons pepper, ½ teaspoons salt, ½ cup mozzarella and herbs. In a separate bowl mix together the egg, salt and ricotta and pour over the pasta mixture. Gently stir until combined. Pour into a greased 8 inch square baking dish, top with the remaining mozzarella and place to bake in your preheated oven at 400° for until bubbly and browned (should take about 15 minutes).

6) Greek Pasta with Meatballs

This tasty pasta and meatball dish uses a rice shaped pasta and tangy feta cheese paired with delicious meatballs that can be frozen stored and used in other exciting creations. This is a must have.

Yield: 4

Cooking Time: 40 minutes

List of Ingredients:

- Hot cooked orzo (2cups)
- Plain dry breadcrumbs (⅓ cup)
- Dried oregano (½ teaspoon)
- Salt (¼ teaspoon)
- Ground cinnamon (¼ teaspoon)
- Freshly ground black pepper (¼ teaspoon)
- Lean ground lamb (1 lb)
- Garlic clove, (1 minced)
- Chopped fresh parsley (2 teaspoon)
- Large egg whites (2)
- Olive oil (1 ½ teaspoons)
- Jarred marinara sauce (2 cups)
- Crumbled feta cheese (¾ cup [3 ounces])

Procedure:

First preheat oven to 375°. Then cook orzo according to the package directions. Drain and place in a container to keep warm. Mix breadcrumbs and next 6 ingredients (through garlic) in a medium bowl. Add 1 ½ teaspoons of parsley and egg whites, stir until thoroughly combined. Use the mixture to form 12 (1 inch) meatballs; put them to chill for 5 minutes. Heat oil over medium heat in a large skillet (ovenproof). Cook meatballs until they are brown on all sides. Drain excess oil from meatballs and wipe pan with paper towels. Place the meatballs back in pan and spoon marinara sauce over them. Sprinkle them with cheese and bake for 11 minutes or until meatballs are done. Serve with orzo. Sprinkle with parsley and enjoy!

7) Peppery Chicken Pasta Salad

Quick, easy and absolutely delicious.

Yield: 4

Cooking Time: 1 Hr. 35 Minutes

List of Ingredients:

Salad:

- Farfalle (3 cups, uncooked)
- Green beans (2 cups)
- Chicken breast (2 cups, rotisserie, chopped)
- Celery (⅔ cup, chopped)
- Bell pepper (1, red, chopped)
- Red onion (½, thinly sliced)

Dressing:

- Water (2 tablespoons)
- Mayonnaise (3 tablespoons, light)
- Lemon juice (4 teaspoons)
- Pesto (4 teaspoons)

- Black pepper (½ teaspoons)
- Salt (¼ teaspoons)

Procedure:

Salad: Place the pasta to cook over medium heat in boiling water until completely cooked. After about 6 minutes add in the green beans and leave it to cook with your pasta for about 5 minutes. Drain pasta then rinse in cold water to stop the cooking process. Combine pasta, chicken, beans, pepper, celery and onion. Gently toss to set aside then set aside. Create your dressing by whisking together 2 tablespoons. Water and remaining ingredients. Drizzle over your pasta, gently toss and serve. Enjoy.

8) Fettuccine with Mushrooms and Hazelnuts

The taste of this vegetarian dish will blow your mind. The nutty aroma and taste of mushroom and hazelnut will surprise and entice your palate. This meatless meal is one guaranteed to satisfy your taste buds.

Yield: 4

Cooking Time: 20 minutes

List of Ingredients:

- Fettuccine (9 oz.)
- Butter (1 teaspoon)
- Blanched Hazelnut (¼ cup chopped)
- Garlic cloves (4, thinly sliced)

- Olive Oil (1 teaspoon)
- Salt (½ teaspoons)
- Freshly ground black pepper (¼ teaspoons)
- Fresh sage (2 teaspoons)
- Parmigiano-Reggiano cheese (2 Oz, shaved)
- Chives (finely chopped, 2 teaspoons)

Procedure:

Cook pasta as directed on package excluding salt then drain. Drain in a colander over and a bowl, reserve about ¾ cup of the liquid from pasta. Melt butter in a large nonstick skillet while the water for the pasta starts to boil. Add the hazelnuts to pan and sauté for 3 minutes till nuts are toasted and fragrance is high. Remove with a slotted spoon and add oil to pan. Add garlic and mushrooms, sprinkle with ¼ teaspoon salt and black pepper. Sauté the mixture for 5 minutes and stir in sage. Add the cooking liquid that was reserved and remaining salt along with pasta; toss to combine. Remove from stove and top with hazelnuts, chives and cheese. Serve and enjoy!

9) Roasted Chicken and Bow Tie Pasta Salad

This is a great for dinner time and the flavors will definitely have you wanting to bring some of the leftovers for lunch.

Yield: 6

Cooking Time: 40 minutes

List of Ingredients:

- Farfalle (3 cups, uncooked)
- Orange juice (⅓ cup)
- Lemon juice (¼ cup)
- Olive oil (2 tablespoons, Extra Virgin)
- Mustard (1 tablespoon)
- Sugar (2 teaspoons)
- Salt (1 ¼ teaspoons)
- Black pepper (½ teaspoons)
- Rice vinegar (1 ½ teaspoons)
- Chicken Brest (2 cups, cooked, shredded)
- Red grapes (1 ½ cups, seedless, halved)
- Celery (1 cup, cut)
- Red onion (1/3 cup, diced)
- Toasted Walnut (1/3 cup, chopped)
- Fresh chives (3 tablespoons, chopped)
- Fresh parsley (2 tablespoons, chopped)

Procedure:

Allow the pasta to cook using the directions on the package and set aside until completely cooled. Now create your dressing by whisking together all the ingredients listed above beginning with the orange juice through to rice vinegar. Finally, pour the mixture onto your pasta then add the celery, chicken, red onion, grapes, nuts, parsley and chives. Gently toss until combined then serve. Enjoy.

10) Peppery Monterey Jack Pasta Salad

This is a quick pasta dish done in about 20 minutes or less and may be had as an entree or side dish. Either way it is packed with tons of flavor and will definitely leave you wanting more.

Yield: 4

Cooking Time: 20 minutes

List of Ingredients:

- Pasta (6 oz. acini di pepe)
- 14 oz. tomato (diced)
- Capers (⅓ cup rinsed, drained)
- Red onion (¼ cup, finely chopped)
- Banana peppers (¼ cup pickled, sliced)
- Fresh parsley (¼ cup, chopped)
- Cider vinegar (2 teaspoons)
- Olive oil (1 tablespoon extra-virgin)
- Dried oregano (½ teaspoons)
- Salt (⅛ teaspoons)
- Monterey Jack cheese (2 Oz, cut into cubes)
- 16 oz. Can Rinsed and drained Navy beans
- Salami, (1oz.chopped)
- Garlic (1 clove diced)

Procedure:

Cook pasta as directed on package excluding salt then drain. In a large bowl combine tomato and remaining ingredients. Add mixture to the pasta and toss well. Next prepare breadsticks. Combine 1 teaspoon black pepper, 1 teaspoon sesame seeds and ½ cup grated Asiago cheese. Cut breadstick dough (7oz) into 8 sticks; roll in cheese mix and bake. Serve pasta and breadsticks and enjoy!

11) Zucchini Fusilli

Stripping the zucchini and cooking it with the pasta makes them cling to each other thus creating a blend. Be sure not to overcook the zucchini though just until tender and bonded with pasta. Added pine nuts add more richness to this dish.

Yield: 6

Cooking Time: 40 minutes

List of Ingredients:
- Zucchini (2 lbs.)
- Garlic (2 cloves)
- Basil Leaves (12, large)
- Pine nuts (⅓ cup)
- Butter (2 tablespoons)
- Olive oil (1 tablespoon)
- Salt (1 tablespoon ½ teaspoons)
- Fusilli (¾ lbs.)

- Parmesan Cheese (1 cup, shredded)

Procedure:
Place a large pot with water over heat to boil and proceed to clean and cut your zucchini then set aside. Next, cut your garlic and basil leaves then set aside. In a skillet, toast the pine nuts on medium heat and set aside. On a high flame melt 1 tablespoon butter in your skillet with 2 teaspoon olive oil then proceed to add a ½ of the zucchini with a ¼ teaspoons salt.

Cook until soft and browned (5 minutes). Take zucchini from pan with a slotted spoon, draining as much oil from it as possible. Add the rest of the zucchini and repeat. Turn flame off reserving pan. Add i tablespoon salt and fusilli to boiling water, cook until tender and drain, put in a large bowl. Put reserved frying pan over medium heat and add 1 teaspoon oil and chopped garlic, cook until fragrance is high; do not brown. Then add zucchini and pine nuts; cook until combined. Add zucchini mixture along with basil to pasta and toss. Add ½ cup parmesan and remaining butter and toss until butter melts and all ingredients are well combined. Serve in bowls and sprinkle with cheese. Eat immediately.

12) Quick-Roasted Cherry Tomato Sauce with Spaghetti

This is a dish for those vegetarians out there, with some fresh items that you may even have in your garden such as cherry tomatoes, basil, and parsley. Add some goat cheese for a truly divine taste; this is both quick and delicious.

Yield: 4

Cooking Time: 32 minutes

List of Ingredients:

- Water (4qts)
- Kosher salt (2 teaspoons)
- Uncooked spaghetti (8oz)
- Tomatoes (cherry, 2 ⅔ cups)
- Olive oil (Extra-virgin, 2 tablespoons)
- Vinegar (Red wine, 2 teaspoons)
- Red pepper (Crushed, ⅛ teaspoons)
- Basil leaves (2 ½ tablespoons Chopped)
- Flat-leaf parsley (2 ½ tablespoons Chopped)
- Semi Soft goat cheese (Crumbled, 2oz)

Procedure:

Heat oven to 450°. Boil the water including salt and add spaghetti and cook for ten minutes or until spaghetti is medium done. Drain in a colander over a bowl and reserve ⅓ cup of the water it was cooked in. Cover in pan to keep warm. Combine in a jelly roll pan: tomatoes, 1 teaspoon oil, vinegar, salt and pepper; spread evenly in pan. Bake tomatoes until they are soft and charred lightly in place. Then in a Dutch oven put tomatoes and tomato juice into spaghetti. Use 3 tablespoons of water reserved from cooking pasta to loosen browned bits in jelly-roll pan. Carefully pour water mixture and remaining teaspoon of oil into spaghetti mix. Over medium flame place Dutch oven and add remaining water from cooking, using a tablespoon at a time, until spaghetti mix is moist, tossing constantly. Stir basil and parsley into pasta mix. Sprinkle with cheese. Serve and enjoy!

13) Pasta with Asparagus, Pancetta, and Pine Nuts

Lemon juice and fresh asparagus bring much flavor to this recipe. The pine nuts are particularly delicious, but feel free to use walnuts instead if you have them on hand.

Yield: 4

Cooking Time:

List of Ingredients:

- Cavatappi pasta (8 oz., Uncooked)
- Asparagus (1 lb., trimmed and cut)
- Garlic (1 teaspoon, minced)
- Pine nuts (3 tablespoons)
- Pancetta (2 oz., diced)
- Lemon juice (2 tablespoons)
- Olive oil (2 teaspoons, Extra Virgin)
- Salt (½ teaspoons)
- Black pepper (¼ teaspoons)
- Parmigiano-Reggiano cheese (¼ cup, Crumbled)

Procedure:

Set your oven to preheat at 400°. Allow your pasta to cook as directed by the container without adding any salt or additional fat. About 3 minutes before the pasta is completely cooked, add your asparagus and allow cooking. Drain the pasta and asparagus from the pot, add a bit of garlic to the mixture and toss. Line your jelly roll pan with a layer of nuts. Allow baking at 400° r until golden and fragrant (should be about 3 minutes while occasionally stirring.

Transfer the contents over to a smaller bowl then increase the oven temperature to 475°. Add your pancetta on the jelly roll pan and allow baking until crisp (should be about 6 minutes). In a separate bowl proceed to mix together the lemon juice, salt, olive oil and pepper then whisk until completely combined. Use this lemon mixture to drizzle over your pasta then top with the pine nuts, cheese and pancetta. Serve and enjoy.

14) Roasted Butternut Squash and Bacon Pasta

The richness of butternut squash is complimented well with smoky bacon in this tasty family meal. You may also use mini penne pasta as it's about the same size as the squash or you may also use elbow macaroni or shell pasta.

Yield: 5

Cooking Time: 90 minutes

List of Ingredients:

- Salt (¾ teaspoons)
- Rosemary (½ teaspoons dried)
- Black pepper (Freshly ground, ¼ teaspoons)
- Butternut squash (3 cups, peeled and cubed)
- Cooking spray
- Bacon (6 slices, raw/Sweet hickory smoked)
- Shallots (1 cup sliced thinly)
- Uncooked mini penne (8 oz.)
- All-purpose flour (¼ cup)
- Reduced-fat milk (2 cups)
- Cheese (¾ cup, Sharp provolone /shredded)
- Fresh Parmesan cheese (1/3 cup, grated)

Procedure:

Set oven to 425°. Mix together ¼ teaspoon salt, pepper and rosemary. Then line a baking pan with foil and coat with cooking spray. Put squash onto foil and sprinkle with salt mix. Bake for 45 minutes until tender and browned lightly. Turn oven temperature up to 450°. In a large nonstick skillet over medium heat put bacon and cook until crisp. Take bacon out from pan; leave 1 ½ teaspoon of drippings in pan, crumble bacon. Add shallots and sauté for 8 minutes until it is tender. Combine squash mix, bacons and shallot and set aside. Prepare pasta as directed on package excluding salt then drain. Mix flour and ½ teaspoon In a Dutch oven over medium heat. Add milk gradually, constantly stirring with a whisk. Cook until it thickens slightly, constantly stirring. Once thickened take pan from heat. Add provolone to the mix and stir till cheese melts. Add pasta to cheese mix and toss well. Coat a 11 x 7 baking dish with cooking spray and spoon into pan and top with squash mix. Use Parmesan cheese to sprinkle evenly and bake for 10 minutes. Serve and Enjoy!!!

15) Orecchiette with Peas, Shrimp, and Buttermilk-Herb Dressing

This herb pasta salad is good for a picnic, increase ingredients if you like and make for a crowd. Orecchiette can be substituted with medium shell pasta. Creamy, herby and delicious...yum!!

Yield: 4

Cooking Time: 30 minutes

List of Ingredients:
- Orecchiette pasta (8 oz..)
- Green Peas (1 cup, shelled)
- Shrimp (½ lb, medium, peeled, deveined)
- Radishes (1 cup, sliced)
- Mayonnaise (⅓ cup, low fat)
- Buttermilk (¼ cup)
- Chives (3 tablespoons, minced)
- Dill (1 tablespoon, chopped)
- Salt (½ teaspoons)
- Lemon rind (½ teaspoons, grated)
- Lemon juice (1 tablespoon)
- Black pepper (¼ teaspoons)
- Red pepper (⅛ teaspoons)
- Garlic (2 cloves, minced)

Procedure:
Allow the pasta to cook using the directions on the package. When there is about 2 minutes left add the shrimp and peas to finish cooking with the pasta. Drain the pasta and rinse with cold water to freeze the cooking process. Next, add radishes to the pasta mixture and toss until combined fully. In a separate bowl, whisk together the remaining ingredients and use to coat the pasta. Allow to stand covered for at least 20 minutes. Serve chilled or at room temperature. Enjoy.

16) Sausage, Tomato, and Arugula Fettuccine

This is a dish that is easy to prepare and has a very bold taste from its ingredients. Savory sausage and peppery arugula along with Romano cheese complement each other well in this dish.

Yield: 4

Cooking Time: 20 minutes

List of Ingredients:

- 1 Package fettuccine (9oz, refrigerated)
- Olive oil (1 tablespoon)
- Turkey sausage (6 ounces, Italian)
- Garlic (2 teaspoons, diced)
- Cherry tomatoes (1 pint)
- Black pepper (¼ teaspoon)
- Arugula leaves (baby, 3 cups)
- Pecorino Romano cheese (2 Oz, shaved)

Procedure:

Cook pasta as directed on package excluding salt then drain. Save ⅔ cup liquid from cooking. Then In a large skillet heat oil over medium heat. Take casing from sausage and break into small pieces. And cook in pan for 3 minutes. Stir constantly so as to crumble. Then add garlic; cook for 30 seconds. Add pepper and tomatoes, cover pan and allow to cook for two minutes. After the tomatoes have been cooked, mash them with a spoon. Lower the heat and cover pan allowing to cook for. Take skillet from heat, put pasta, liquid from cooking and arugula and toss. Sprinkle with Romano and serve.

17) Bow Ties with Tomatoes, Feta, and Balsamic Dressing

This is an easy to make pasta salad and very healthy. Not to fret as it is not in the least a bland dish. Its surprise ingredient of green grapes adds an interesting element and flavor to compliment the tomatoes and feta. Finish it off by serving with pan grilled asparagus.

Yield: 4

Cooking Time: 1 Hour

List of Ingredients:

- 6 oz. Farfalle
- Grape tomatoes (2 cups, halved)
- Green grapes (1 cup, halved/seedless)
- Basil leaves (⅓ cup sliced thin)
- Balsamic White Vinegar (2 tablespoons)
- Shallots (2 tablespoons, cut)
- Capers (2 teaspoons)
- Mustard (1 teaspoon Dijon)
- Bottled garlic (½ teaspoon, minced)
- Salt (½ teaspoon)
- Black pepper (¼ teaspoon)
- Olive oil (4 teaspoons)
- 1 package of Crumbled feta cheese (reduced-fat)

Procedure:

(For Pasta)

Cook pasta as directed on package excluding salt then drain. In a large bowl combine pasta, grapes, tomatoes and basil. In a small bowl mix vinegar and the six ingredients that follow (down to pepper), whisk and drizzle over pasta mixture. Then add cheese and toss.

(For Grilled asparagus)

In a large bowl blend together 1 teaspoon of oil, ¼ teaspoons of salt, 1/8 teaspoon of freshly ground black pepper and one (1) lb. asparagus that has been trimmed. Get a grill pan and put it over a medium flame. Use cooking spray to coat the pan. Put asparagus into pan and cook for 5 minutes till it is supple, turning at least once.

Pair pasta with asparagus, serve and enjoy.

18) Whole-Wheat Spaghetti with Arugula

This healthy dish is not only easy to make but is cheap and very tasty. Arugula leaves that have matured in the summer's heat tend to be hot and spicy. What more can i saw another flavorful pasta delight for healthy eaters or vegetarians.

Yield: 4

Cooking Time: 20 minutes

List of Ingredients:

- Olive oil (2 tablespoons)
- Red pepper (¼ teaspoons, crushed)
- Garlic cloves (2, diced)
- Tomato (1 cup, minced)
- 1lb arugula (trimmed, torn)
- 8 oz. spaghetti (whole wheat)
- Vinegar (1 ½ tablespoons Red wine)
- Salt (¾ teaspoons)
- Black pepper (½ teaspoons, freshly ground)
- Parmesan cheese (½ cup, grated)

Procedure:

Cook pasta as directed on package excluding salt then drain. Then over medium flame in a deep frying pot, heat 1 tablespoon oil. Then put pepper and garlic and sauté for 20 seconds. Then put in tomato and arugula and allow to cook until arugula is blanched. Put mixture In a large bowl out and add following List of Ingredients: a tablespoon of oil, spaghetti, salt, vinegar, and black pepper; toss well. Use cheese to sprinkle over pasta. Serve and enjoy.

19) Roasted Asparagus and Tomato Penne Salad with Goat Cheese

Want to be the star of your next dinner party? Then try this upscale pasta salad, ingredients combined to impress whoever has a taste. Can be served immediately or chilled; either way it will be a 'fave'.

Yield: 4

Cooking Time: 35 minutes

List of Ingredients:
- Penne (2 cups)
- Asparagus (12, spears)
- Tomatoes (12)
- Olive oil (4 tablespoons)
- Kosher salt (⅜ teaspoon)
- Black pepper (½ teaspoons)
- Shallots (1 tablespoon, diced)
- Lemon juice (2 teaspoons, freshly squeezed)
- Mustard (1 tablespoon, Dijon)
- Herbes de Provence (1 teaspoon, dried)

- Honey (1 ½ teaspoon)
- Kalamata olives (½ cup pitted, halved)
- Baby arugula (2 cups)
- Goat cheese (½ cup, crumbled)

Procedure:
Set oven to 400°. Cook pasta as directed on package excluding salt and fat, drain and cover in a container. Get a jelly roll pan and put asparagus and tomatoes in it. Drizzle with a tablespoon of olive oil and sprinkle with ¼ teaspoon of salt and ¼ teaspoon of black pepper. Gently toss to coat; organize asparagus and tomato mixture to form a single layer. Bake at 400° for 6 minutes till the asparagus is crisp-tender. Take asparagus from pan. Put pan in oven, and bake tomatoes for an extra 4 minutes. Take tomatoes from pan and let tomatoes and asparagus allow to cool for 10 minutes. Then cut asparagus into one inch lengths and cut tomatoes in halves. Then get a small bowl and blend shallots and other four ingredients (through to honey). Whisk and add remaining three teaspoons oil, ⅛ teaspoon of salt and ¼ black pepper. Place pasta, olives, asparagus, tomato and arugula in a big bowl and toss. Drizzle mix over pasta mixture and toss. Use cheese to sprinkle over pasta and serve.

20) Farfalle with Tomatoes, Onions, and Spinach

Give your family a taste of the Mediterranean with this nutritious meatless pasta dish. You may add chicken if you desire; be warned, leftovers will not be spared either way.

Yield: 4

Cooking Time: 40 minutes

List of Ingredients:

- Salt (1 ¼ teaspoon)
- Uncooked farfalle pasta (8 oz.)
- Extra-virgin olive oil (2 tablespoons)
- Yellow onion (1 cup vertically sliced)
- Dried oregano (1 teaspoon)
- Garlic (5 cloves, sliced)
- Grape tomatoes (2 cups, halved)
- White wine vinegar (1 tablespoon)
- Baby spinach (3 cups)
- Fresh Parmigiano-Reggiano cheese (3 tablespoons shaved)
- Freshly ground black pepper (¼ teaspoon)
- Crumbled feta cheese (¾ cup)

Procedure:

Cook pasta as directed on package using 1 tablespoon salt then drain. Heat 1 tablespoon oil in a large nonstick skillet and add onion and oregano. Sauté until lightly browned then add tomatoes and vinegar. Sauté the mixture until tomatoes begin to get soft. Add pasta and spinach and cook for a minute. Remove from heat and stir in Parmigiano-Reggiano and remaining oil along with salt and pepper. Sprinkle with feta and serve.

21) Mushroom Bolognese

This dish is bursting with flavor from all angles. Freshly ground pork and earthy mushrooms all in a creamy sauce. Certainly will be a highlight for you and very fulfilling. Your palate will certainly thank you.

Yield: 6

Cooking Time: 1hr 10 minutes

List of Ingredients:

- Porcini mushrooms (½ Oz, dried)
- 1 cup boiled water
- Olive oil (1 tablespoon)
- Onion (2 ½ cups chopped)
- Kosher salt (¾ teaspoon)
- Black pepper (½ teaspoon)
- Ground pork (½ pound)
- Cremini mushrooms (8 cups, chopped finely)
- Garlic (1 tablespoon minced)
- Tomato paste (2 tablespoons)
- White wine (½ cup)
- 1 can whole tomatoes (peeled)
- Whole milk (¼ cup)
- Whole wheat spaghetti (10oz.)
- Salt (1 tablespoon)
- Cheese (1 ½ oz., Parmigiano, grated)
- Fresh parsley (¼ cup chopped)

Procedure:
Put porcini with boiled water inside a bowl, cover and set aside for 20 minutes till they get soft. Using a colander, drain porcini over a container. Keep liquid to be used later. Rinse porcini and chop. In a large deep-frying pan heat oil over medium flame. Then add ½ teaspoon of salt, ¼ teaspoon of pepper, onion and pork. Allow to cook for 10 minutes till pork is brown, stirring to break up pork. Put mushrooms, garlic, remainder of salt (¼ teaspoons), and ¼ teaspoon pepper to pan. Allow to cook for 15 minutes until liquid almost dries out, stir periodically. Add porcini; and cook for a minute. Then add tomato paste and allow to cook for 2 minutes, stirring regularly. Pour liquid from porcini and wine into pot and cook for a minute, scrape pan to loosen bits that have been browned. Add tomatoes and allow to boil. Reduce heat and allow to cook for 30 minutes. Stir to break up tomatoes and stir in milk, allow to cook for two minutes. Cook pasta as directed on package using a tablespoon of salt to boiling water. Drain and mix pasta with sauce. Sprinkle with parsley and cheese. Serve and enjoy!

22) Wax Bean, Roasted Pepper, and Tomato Pasta with Goat Cheese

A variety of different tastes that blend together to tantalize your taste buds. A tart vinaigrette compliments sweet bell peppers and a taste of goat cheese to add dimension. Quite a

Yield: 8

Cooking Time: 40 minutes

List of Ingredients:

- 1 medium Red bell pepper
- Fettuccine pasta (8oz, uncooked)
- Water (2 quarts)
- Salt (2 ½ teaspoons)
- 1-pound wax beans, trimmed and cut in half crosswise
- Cherry tomatoes (2 cups, halved)
- Green onions (½ cup sliced)
- Fresh parsley (¼ cup chopped)
- Cider vinegar (2 tablespoons)
- Fresh lemon juice (2 tablespoons)
- Dijon mustard (1 tablespoon)
- Sugar (1 ½ teaspoons)
- Extra virgin olive oil (1 teaspoon)
- Crumbled goat cheese (½ cup)

Procedure:

Cook pasta as directed on package excluding salt and fat, drain. Preheat broiler. Cut the bell pepper in half lengthwise and discard the seeds. Place peppers with skin sides up on a foil lined baking sheet and press with hands. Broil pepper till they get blackened. Place in zip lock bag and seal; let stand for 15 minutes. Boil 2 quarts of water with 2 teaspoon of salt in a large saucepan. Put beans in pan and cook until beans are crisp tender; drain and put in a large bowl. Add bell pepper, tomatoes, onions, parsley and toss to combine. Combine remaining ½ teaspoons salt, vinegar and remaining ingredients excluding goat cheese, whisk and drizzle over salad. Pour mixture on to pasta and toss to combine. Sprinkle with goat cheese. Serve and enjoy.

23) Asparagus and Chicken Carbonara

Traditional carbonara is made with whipping cream and raw egg yolks however this is a much healthier method that can achieved with fat-free evaporated milk and egg substitute. This meal must be had warm though as the sauce gets thick when cold.

Yield: 5

Cooking Time: 25 minutes

List of Ingredients:
- Uncooked spaghetti (8 ounces)
- Asparagus (2 cups, sliced)
- Egg substitute (½ cup)
- Evaporated milk (½ cup, fat free)
- Olive oil (2 teaspoons)
- Onion (½ cup, chopped)

- Dry vermouth (¼ cup)
- Rotisserie chicken breast (2 cups, chopped)
- Fresh Parmesan cheese (½ cup, grated)
- Fresh flat-leaf parsley (3 tablespoons, chopped finely)
- Salt (¾ teaspoon)
- Freshly ground black pepper (½ teaspoon)
- 4 bacon slices (cooked, crumbled)

Procedure:
Bring a pot of water to boil and add pasta and cook till al dente. Asparagus should be added to pot during final 2 minutes of cooking. Drain pasta and asparagus mix in a colander over a bowl. Reserve 1/3 cup cooking liquid and combine with milk and egg substitute, stir with a whisk. Heat oil in a large nonstick skillet over medium flame and add onion to pan; sauté 2 minutes. Then put vermouth in pot; cook for a minute. Put pasta mixture and stir to blend. Remove pasta mix from flame and stir in milk mix, chicken, and cheese. Place pan over medium heat, and allow to cook for 4 minutes until slightly thick, stirring constantly. Remove from heat; stir in parsley, salt, pepper, and bacon. Serve soon after.

24) Penne with Sausage, Eggplant, and Feta

This is quick and hearty dish. A well-rounded dish combining rich breakfast sausage, robust eggplant and vibrant feta cheese. Great for dinner time.

Yield: 4

Cooking Time: 20 minutes

List of Ingredients:

- Peeled and Cubed eggplant (4 ½ cups)
- Pork breakfast sausage (½ lb.)
- Garlic cloves, (4, minced)
- Tomato paste (2 tablespoons)
- Oregano (1 teaspoon, dried)
- Black pepper (¼ teaspoon)
- 1 (14.5 oz.) Can tomatoes (diced)
- 6 cups Penne (hot, cooked)
- Crumbled feta cheese (½ cup)
- Chopped fresh parsley (¼ cup)

Procedure:

Cook eggplant, garlic, and sausage using a large nonstick skillet over medium heat for 5 minutes till the sausage gets brown and eggplant gets tender. Add oregano, tomato paste, black pepper and tomatoes to pan. Allow to cook over medium flame for 5 minutes, stirring occasionally. In a large bowl put pasta and add tomato mix, cheese, and parsley. Toss well to combine. Serve and enjoy.

Part 2

1) Classic Tomato Pasta Sauce

Preparation Time: 10 minutes

Cooking Time: 20 minutes

Ready In: 30 minutes

Servings: 2

INGREDIENTS:

3 medium sized Tomatoes

2 teaspoon Tomato Sauce

4 Garlic cloves

1 small Onion

1/4 teaspoon Oregano

1/2 teaspoon Chilli flakes

1 teaspoon Sugar

1 tablespoon Olive Oil

Salt & Black Pepper as per taste

DIRECTIONS:

1. In a medium sized bowl boil water and add the tomatoes to it. Be careful not to splash any hot water. Let the tomatoes cook in the boiling water for 2 – 3 minutes or until you can see the outer skin peeling off.

2. When the tomatoes reach this stage, remove the pan from the gas and remove the tomatoes from the boiling water. Let them cool and then peel off the

outer skin. Then puree these tomatoes into a fine paste, do not add any water.

3.In a separate medium sized deep and flat saucepan heat the oil and add the chopped onions and garlic to it. Fry them till they turn golden brown.

4.Add the tomato puree to this and stir. Allow it to cook for some time and then bring the sauce to a boil. Boil for about 3 minutes.

5.Now add half cup water to this sauce and stir to combine everything. Allow the water to come to a boil. Boil for at least 2 minutes.

6.Now add the salt, black pepper, oregano, chili flakes, tomato sauce and sugar to this mix and keep stirring till it reaches a sauce consistency. Serve with your choice of pasta!

2) Friulano Cheese & Sour Cream Pasta Sauce

Preparation Time: 3 minutes

Cooking Time: 7 minutes

Ready In: 10 minutes

Servings: 2

INGREDIENTS:

225 grams Friulano cheese, grated

1 cup 35% cream

1/4 cup green onions, sliced thinly

2 cloves garlic, chopped

1 pinch saffron threads

55 grams hazelnuts, toasted, peeled & chopped

2 tablespoons olive oil

Salt and freshly ground pepper as per taste

DIRECTIONS:

1.Place a medium sized deep saucepan over high heat and add the olive oil to it. Once the oil is hot enough, add the onions and garlic and sauté them for about 1 minute on high heat.

2.Now add the sour cream and saffron to this and stir. Cook everything for 2 more minutes.

3.Add the cheese to the saucepan and simmer the flame. Stir the sauce and keep stirring until the cheese melts.

4.Remove the saucepan from the heat once done and add the hazelnuts, salt and pepper to the sauce and stir to mix everything nicely.

5.Pour the sauce over your choice of pasta, toss and serve hot!

3) Vodka & Ham Pasta Sauce

Preparation Time: none

Cooking Time: 10 minutes

Ready In: 10 minutes

Servings: 2

INGREDIENTS:

1/4 cup vodka

115 grams prosciutto (ham), in thin strips

1 can diced tomatoes, with their liquid

1/4 cup 35% cream

1/2 cup onion, chopped

3 cloves garlic, chopped finely

1 tablespoon fresh oregano, chopped

2 tablespoons olive oil

Salt and freshly ground pepper as per taste

DIRECTIONS:

1.Place a medium sized deep saucepan over medium heat and add the olive oil to it. Once the oil is hot enough, add the onions and the ham. Now add the garlic and cook everything for about 1 minute.

2.Now pour the vodka in the saucepan and cook the mixture until the vodka evaporates completely.

3.Now add the tomatoes (with their liquid from the can) and cook the mixture till the entire sauce reduces and thickens slightly. Stir occasionally.4.Now add the cream to this mixture and stir. Cook for about 2 minutes.

5.Season with salt, pepper and oregano and pour over your choice of pasta. Toss and serve!

4) Kalamata Olive & Red Pepper Pasta Sauce

Preparation Time: none

Cooking Time: 10 minutes

Ready In: 10 minutes

Servings: 2

INGREDIENTS:

12 kalamata olives, pitted and quartered

1 teaspoon red pepper, crushed

1/4 onion, chopped

5 cloves garlic, chopped

2 ripe tomatoes, diced

6 sun-dried tomatoes, softened and chopped

1 tablespoon capers

1 pinch dried oregano

1/4 cup olive oil

DIRECTIONS:

1.Place a medium sized deep saucepan over medium heat and add the olive oil to it. Once the oil is hot enough, add the onions, garlic and red pepper and sauté for about 1 minute.

2.Now add the sun dried tomatoes, oregano and capers to this and stir everything. Cook for another minute.

3.Now add the fresh ripe tomatoes and kalamata olives. Cover the saucepan and cook everything for about 5 minutes. Stir occasionally. Pour over your choice of pasta, toss and serve!

5) Bacon & Worcester Pasta Sauce

Preparation Time: 3 minutes
Cooking Time: 37 minutes
Ready In: 40 minutes
Servings: 4

INGREDIENTS:

120 grams streaky bacon

Dash of Worcester sauce

1 small can chopped tomatoes

1 onion, thinly sliced

1 dried chilli, seeds discarded and chopped finely

1 teaspoon sugar

3 tablespoons olive oil

Salt and Pepper as per taste

DIRECTIONS:

1. Place a medium sized frying pan on low heat and add the olive oil to it. Meanwhile, slice the bacon into pieces of about 7mm thickness.

2. Once the oil is hot enough, add the bacon slices to it and cook on low heat until the bacon starts to become crispy on the edges.

3. Now add the onion slices and chopped chili and cook on low heat for about 15 minutes or until the onions start to caramelize.

4. Now add the chopped tomatoes and sugar to this and let the mixture cook on low-medium heat for about 15 – 20 minutes. This will thicken the sauce.

5. Now season the sauce with salt, pepper and dash of Worcester sauce and stir. Pour on pasta of your choice and serve!

6) Half-and-Half & Butternut Squash Pasta Sauce

Preparation Time: 20 minutes

Cooking Time: 40 minutes

Ready In: 1 hour

Servings: 8

INGREDIENTS:

1 cup half-and-half

1 medium butternut squash

5 cloves garlic, peel on

1/2 teaspoon dried rubbed sage

1 tablespoon olive oil

Coarse salt and ground pepper as per taste

DIRECTIONS:

1. Start with the butternut squash first. Trim the ends of the squash using a sharp knife. Cut the squash into half from the middle. Now peel both ends with a peeler and cut them into halves again. Lastly, scoop out the seeds using a spoon.

2. Cut the prepared squash into 2 – inch pieces and place them on a small rimmed baking sheet. Toss these squash pieces with oil and sage and sprinkle salt and pepper on them. Toss again to coat evenly.

3. Preheat the oven to 375 degrees and place the garlic cloves around the squash pieces on the baking sheet.

Bake for about 40 minutes or until the squash becomes very tender, tossing after 20 minutes. When done, remove the sheet from the oven and peel off the garlic skin.

4. Now put the garlic and squash into a food processor / grinder and puree them. Stop processing and pour the half-and-half in the processor and puree again until the mixture becomes smooth.

5. Add 1 – 2 cups of water and blend again. The final consistency of the sauce should be smooth but not runny. Add water when required and keep blending to achieve this consistency.

6. Finally season the sauce with salt. Pour over your choice of pasta, toss and serve!

7) Green Herbs & Cheese Pasta Sauce

Preparation Time: none

Cooking Time: 15 minutes

Ready In: 15 minutes

Servings: 4 – 6

INGREDIENTS:

4 tablespoons fresh parsley, chopped

2 tablespoons fresh basil, whole

1 package cream cheese, softened

1/3 cup parmesan cheese, grated

1/4 cup butter, softened

1 garlic clove, minced

1/4 cup olive oil

1/2 teaspoon pepper

2/3 cup boiling water

DIRECTIONS:

1. Place a medium sized saucepan over medium heat and melt the butter in it.

2. Add basil, parsley and garlic to this and cook for about a minute.

3. Add the cream cheese and parmesan cheese to this mixture and cook till the cheese melts. Now add the olive oil and pepper and stir nicely.

4. Now add the boiling water to this mixture stirring continuously. Mix everything well and simmer the flame. Let the sauce cook on simmer flame for 5 minutes. Keep stirring.

5. Pour on your choice of pasta and toss gently. Serve!

8) Anchovy, Tomatoes & Olives Pasta Sauce (Puttanesca)

Preparation Time: none

Cooking Time: 15 minutes

Ready In: 15 minutes

Servings: 4

INGREDIENTS:

1 tin flat anchovy fillets, drained

1 can diced tomatoes, drained

1 can chunky style tomatoes, crushed

20 oil-cured black olives, cracked away from pit and coarsely chopped

4 to 6 garlic cloves, chopped

1/2 teaspoon red pepper flakes, crushed

3 tablespoons capers

1/4 cup flat leaf parsley, chopped

2 tablespoons extra-virgin olive oil

A few grinds black pepper

DIRECTIONS:

1. Place a large deep frying pan over medium heat and add the olive oil to it for heating. Once the oil is hot enough, add the anchovies, garlic and crushed pepper.

2. Cook for about 3 minutes or until the anchovies dissolve into the oil and the garlic becomes tender.

3. Now add the black pepper, parsley, olives, tomatoes and capers. Stir everything and bring it to a boil. Once bubbles start to form, reduce the heat and heat on low flame for 8 – 10 minutes.

4. Pour over your choice of pasta. Toss to coat evenly and serve!

9) Cheese, Nutmeg & Whipping Cream Pasta Sauce (Alfredo)

Preparation Time: none

Cooking Time: 15 minutes

Ready In: 15 minutes

Servings: 2

INGREDIENTS:

1/4 cup grated Parmesan cheese

1/4 cup grated Romano cheese

8 fluid ounces heavy whipping cream

1 pinch ground nutmeg

3 tablespoons butter

1 egg yolk

Salt as per taste

DIRECTIONS:

1. Place a medium sized deep saucepan over medium heat and melt the butter in it.

2. Once the butter melts, add the whipping cream stirring constantly.

3. Now add both grated cheese, salt and nutmeg to the butter and cream mixture and stir nicely. Cook till the cheese melts stirring constantly.

4. Now add the egg yolk to this mixture and stir. Reduce the flame and simmer the sauce over medium-low heat for 3 to 5 minutes.

5. Pour over your choice of pasta, toss and serve!

10) Mushroom & Bell Pepper Pasta Sauce

Preparation Time: none

Cooking Time: 15 minutes

Ready In: 15 minutes

Servings: 8

INGREDIENTS:

1 1/2 cups fresh sliced mushrooms

1/2 cup red bell pepper, chopped

1/2 cup chopped green bell pepper

1 can cream of chicken soup, condensed

1/2 cup chopped onion

1/3 cup milk

4 tablespoons butter

DIRECTIONS:

1. Place a medium sized deep saucepan over medium heat and melt the butter in it.

2. Now add the mushrooms, onions and bell peppers to the melted butter and cook until the mushrooms become tender.

3. Now pour the cream of chicken soup and milk stirring gently while you pour. Cook the sauce until it turns to smooth consistency.

4. Pour over your choice of pasta, toss and serve!

11) Multi Veggie Pasta Sauce (Primavera)

Preparation Time: none

Cooking Time: 25 minutes

Ready In: 25 minutes

Servings: 4

INGREDIENTS:

1 large carrot peeled and sliced into strips

1 red bell pepper, cleaned, seeded and cut into strips

1 cup sliced button mushrooms

1/2 pound thin asparagus, trimmed and cut into 2-inch pieces

1 cup grape or cherry tomatoes, sliced in 1/2

1 cup low-sodium chicken stock

1 tablespoon all-purpose flour, dissolved in 3 tablespoons water

3 cloves minced garlic

1/2 cup 1 percent milk

1 tablespoon olive oil

Salt & Black pepper as per taste

DIRECTIONS:

1. Place a medium sized deep saucepan over medium heat and add the olive oil to it. Once the oil is hot enough add the garlic and cook for about a minute or until the garlic becomes soft.

2. Add the peppers and cook for about 3 minutes or until they start to soften.

3. Now add the tomatoes, mushrooms and asparagus and cook until everything is softened. This will take about 5 minutes.

4. Now pour the dissolved flour and cook for 1 minute.

5. To this mixture add the chicken stock, milk, salt and pepper and bring the sauce to a boil.

6. Reduce the flame and let the sauce simmer for about 5 minutes stirring occasionally. This will thicken the sauce lightly.

7. Now add the carrot strips and stir the sauce nicely. Pour over your choice of pasta, toss and serve!

12) Jarlsberg, Bocconcini & Blue Cheese Pasta Sauce

Preparation Time: none
Cooking Time: 20 minutes
Ready In: 20 minutes
Servings: 4

INGREDIENTS:

125 grams Jarlsberg cheese, cut into small cubes

100 grams Bocconcini cheese, cut into small pieces

60 grams Blue cheese, crumbled

1 brown onion, finely chopped

1 garlic clove, crushed

1 tablespoon chopped fresh tarragon

80 grams butter

1 tablespoon olive oil

Salt & freshly ground pepper as per taste

DIRECTIONS:

1. Place a medium sized deep saucepan over medium heat and add the olive oil to it. Once the oil is hot enough add the garlic and onion and cook for about 7 – 8 minutes or until they becomes very soft.

2.Add the butter to this and stir until it melts. Now add the three cheeses and stir constantly until the cheese melts.

3.Now add the salt and pepper and cook the sauce for another minute. Pour over your choice of pasta, toss and serve!

13) Artichoke & Lemon Pasta Sauce

Preparation Time: 5 minutes

Cooking Time: none

Ready In: 5 minutes

Servings: 4

INGREDIENTS:
1 small jar artichokes

1/4 cup lemon juice

1/4 cup coriander

1/2 teaspoon cayenne pepper

2 medium garlic cloves

1 cup walnuts

1/3 cup extra-virgin olive oil

1/3 cup canola oil

Salt as per taste

DIRECTIONS:

1.Place the garlic cloves, coriander, lemon juice, walnuts, both oils, pepper and salt in a food processor and blend till everything becomes smooth.

2.Now break up the artichokes gently and add to the sauce. No more blending is needed.

3.Pour over your choice of pasta, toss and serve!

14) Broccoli & Garlic Pasta Sauce

Preparation Time: none

Cooking Time: 10 minutes

Ready In: 10 minutes

Servings: 2

INGREDIENTS:

3 cups broccoli florets

3 minced garlic cloves

1/2 teaspoon red-pepper flakes

1/2 cup cream

1/2 cup chicken stock

1/4 cup extra-virgin olive oil

DIRECTIONS:

1.Place a medium sized frying pan over medium heat and add the oil to it for heating. Once the oil is hot enough add the garlic cloves to it. Cook till the garlic turns golden.

2.Now add the broccoli and red pepper flakes to this and cook for about 2 minutes.

3.Pour the chicken stock on this carefully and stir. Cook for about a minute.

4.Now add the cream and stir continuously. Reduce the flame and simmer the sauce for about 5 minutes.

5.Pour over your choice of pasta, toss and serve!

15) Chili Prawns Pasta Sauce

Preparation Time: 15 minutes

Cooking Time: 10 minutes

Ready In: 25 minutes

Servings: 2

INGREDIENTS:

200 grams large raw prawns

1 teaspoon chilli flakes

1 onion, chopped

2 garlic cloves, crushed

1 medium sized tin chopped tomatoes

1/2 tsp golden caster sugar

2 tablespoons Olive oil

DIRECTIONS:

1.In a large bowl pour 1 tablespoon olive oil and add the chilies and half of the garlic to it. Now add the prawns to this and mix to coat the prawns nicely. Let the prawns get marinated in this mix for some time.

2.Place a large frying pan over medium heat and add 1 tablespoon oil to it. Once the oil is hot enough, add the onions and the rest of the garlic to it and cook for about 3 minutes.

3. Now add the tomatoes and sugar to this mixture and stir. Reduce the flame and simmer for 15 minutes.

4. Add the prawns and the marinade to this and cook for 2 minutes or until the prawns turn pink.

5. Pour sauce over your choice of pasta and toss nicely. Serve!

16) Herbs & White Bean Pasta Sauce

Preparation Time: 10 minutes

Cooking Time: 30 minutes

Ready In: 40 minutes

Servings: 2

INGREDIENTS:

1/3 cup Fresh herbs

1 cup dry white beans

1/2 cup Vegetable Stock

1/2 cup Parmesan Cheese

1 can stewed tomatoes, including liquid

1 tablespoon Olive oil

2 – 3 cups Water

Salt and pepper as per taste

DIRECTIONS:

1. Place a medium sized frying pan on medium-high heat and add the olive oil to it. Once the oil is very hot, toss the beans in. Toast the beans in the oil for 2 – 3 minutes.

2. Pour water in the pan such that the beans are completely covered and turn the flame to high. Add salt and pepper to this and simmer the beans until they turn soft. Add water as and when needed.

3. When beans are soft enough, strain them but do not discard the liquid just yet.

4.Now add the beans and the vegetable stock to a food processor and puree. Achieve the consistency of tomato sauce adding the liquid from the beans to thicken and the stock to make the puree thinner when required.

5.Chop the tomatoes into large pieces and add these and the herbs into the sauce right before serving!

17) Capers & Tuna Pasta Sauce

Preparation Time: 10 minutes

Cooking Time: none

Ready In: 10 minutes

Servings: 2

INGREDIENTS:

2 tablespoons capers, drained

1 can tuna (chunk or solid in olive oil), drained

2 tablespoons fresh lemon juice

Grated zest of 1 medium lemon

1 large garlic clove, finely chopped

1/4 cup fresh flat-leaf parsley, chopped

1/4 cup fruity olive oil

Freshly grated Parmesan cheese

Freshly ground black pepper & salt as per taste

DIRECTIONS:

1.In a medium sized bowl place the tuna broken into large bite-sized pieces.

2.Add the lemon zest, garlic, olive oil, lemon juice, capers, salt and pepper and stir gently to combine.

3.Pour water in a deep pot and place the bowl with the tuna over this pot while heating the water. Once the water comes to a boil, remove the bowl.

4.

Add the parmesan cheese and parsley to the sauce and immediately pour over your choice of pasta. Toss and serve!

18) White wine & Clam Pasta Sauce

Preparation Time: none

Cooking Time: 35 minutes

Ready In: 35 minutes

Servings: 4

INGREDIENTS:

3/4 cup dry white wine

50 – 55 small clams, rinsed and scrubbed

4 garlic cloves, thinly sliced

1 medium onion, finely chopped

3 tablespoons olive oil

1/4 teaspoon red-pepper flakes

1/4 cup fresh parsley, coarsely chopped

2 tablespoons butter

Coarse salt

DIRECTIONS:

1. Place a heavy frying pan over medium heat and add the olive oil to it. Once the oil is hot, add the onions, pepper flakes and garlic to it and cook for 5 – 7 minutes or until the onions become soft. Stir occasionally.

2. Now add the wine and bring it to a boil. Cook for about 2 minutes till the sauce is reduced to half. Stir occasionally.

3. Now add the clams and cover the pan. Simmer the clams in the sauce shaking the covered pan

occasionally until the clams open wide. This should take about 3 – 5 minutes. Discard any clams that have not opened up after 5 minutes.

4. Remove the sauce from the heat and add the butter and parsley and season with salt.

5. Pour sauce over your choice of pasta. Toss and serve!

19) Eggs, French Beans & Vinaigrette Pasta Sauce (Niçoise)

Preparation Time: 15 minutes

Cooking Time: none

Ready In: 15 minutes

Servings: 8 (as a side dish)

INGREDIENTS:

200 grams French beans, trimmed and blanched

3 eggs, boiled, peeled and cut into wedges

8 tablespoons ready-made vinaigrette

200 grams can tuna, drained and flaked

150 grams black olives

300 grams cherry tomatoes, halved

1 red onion, sliced

1 garlic clove, crushed

3 tablespoons chopped fresh parsley

DIRECTIONS:

1. In a medium sized bowl combine the French beans, olives, tomatoes, egg wedges, tuna and red onion.

2. Now add the vinaigrette, garlic and parsley and toss everything to coat evenly.

3. Pour this sauce over your choice of pasta and serve!

20) Lime, Cream & Tequila Pasta Sauce

Preparation Time: 5 minutes

Cooking Time: 15 minutes

Ready In: 20 minutes

Servings: 4

INGREDIENTS:

1/2 cup tequila

1/2 cup lime juice

1 1/2 cups cream, plus 2 tablespoons extra

1 shallot, finely minced

1/4 cup white wine vinegar

3 garlic cloves, minced or pressed

1 teaspoon cornstarch

3 tablespoons butter

DIRECTIONS:

1. Place a medium sized deep saucepan over medium-low heat and add the lime juice, vinegar, tequila, shallot and garlic. Cook everything until the quantity reduces to about 1/4 cup.

2. Now add the cream and cook until it is reduced by half. If you prefer, strain out the garlic and shallots.

3. Now place the sauce over the heat again and add the butter.

4.In a small bowl mix the cornstarch with 1 tablespoon water and add to the sauce to thicken it.

5.Pour the sauce over pasta of your choice. Toss and serve!

21) Olive oil & Garlic Pasta Sauce

Preparation Time: none

Cooking Time: 5 minutes

Ready In: 5 minutes

Servings: 2

INGREDIENTS:

1/3 cup extra-virgin olive oil

1 tablespoon garlic, finely chopped

1/4 cup flat-leaf parsley, chopped

Salt as per taste

DIRECTIONS:

1. Place a small deep saucepan over medium-high heat and combine all the ingredients.

2. Once the garlic starts to sizzle, remove the sauce from the heat and pour over your choice of pasta. Toss and serve!

22) Beef & Celery Pasta Sauce

Preparation Time: none

Cooking Time: 2 hours 30 minutes

Ready In: 2 hours 30 minutes

Servings: 7

INGREDIENTS:

2 pounds ground beef

2 ribs celery, finely chopped

1/4 cup chopped pancetta

1 carrot, finely chopped

1 onion, finely chopped

1/2 cup dry red wine

1 clove garlic, finely chopped

1 Can tomato puree

1/4 cup extra-virgin olive oil

Salt and pepper

DIRECTIONS:

1. Place a large heavy deep saucepan over medium-low heat and add the olive oil to it. Once the oil is hot enough add the pancetta and cook for about 5 minutes or until the fat is rendered.

2. Increase the heat to medium and add the onions, celery and carrots and cook for 7 – 8 minutes stirring occasionally until everything becomes soft.

3. Now add the garlic and cook for about 1 minute.

4. Add the beef and increase the heat to medium-high. Cook the beef breaking it up for about 8 minutes or until it is no longer pink.

5. Now pour the wine into this mixture and cook until it completely evaporates. About 5 minutes.

6. Now add the tomato puree and water. Season with salt and bring the sauce to a simmer. Partially cover the pan and cook over low heat for about 2 hours. Stir occasionally during the last 30 minutes. Season the sauce with more salt and pepper if needed.

7. Pour the sauce over pasta of your choice, toss and serve!

23) Spinach & Parmesan Pasta Sauce

Preparation Time: none

Cooking Time: 15 minutes

Ready In: 15 minutes

Servings: 3 – 4

INGREDIENTS:

2 – 3 handfuls spinach

1/2 cup parmesan

2 sprigs thyme (or rosemary)

4 tablespoons butter

2 cloves garlic, minced

DIRECTIONS:

1. Place a medium sized saucepan over medium heat and melt the butter in it.
2. Add the minced garlic to the butter and sauté for 1 minute.
3. Now add the thyme and cook for another minute.
4. Add the spinach and cook till the spinach welts.
5. Now add the parmesan cheese to the sauce and heat till the cheese melts. Stir everything and immediately pour over your choice of pasta. Toss and serve!

24) Sea Food Pasta Sauce

Preparation Time: none

Cooking Time: 1 hour

Ready In: 1 hour

Servings: 6

INGREDIENTS:

2 shallots, minced

8 ounces squid rings

8 ounces bay scallops

4 ounces shrimp (peeled and tails removed)

3/4 cup red wine (Dry, Cab, Zin or Syrah)

3 cups Tomatoes, diced

4 tablespoons olive oil, divided

8 garlic cloves, minced

3 ounces tomato paste, half can

8 ounces tomato sauce

1 teaspoon crushed red pepper flakes

1 tablespoon fresh parsley, chopped

1 tablespoon fresh basil, chopped

Salt and Pepper as per taste

DIRECTIONS:

1. Place a large saucepan over medium heat and add 2 tablespoons olive oil to it for heating. Once the oil is hot enough, add the garlic and shallots.

2. As soon as the garlic starts to sizzle, add the tomato sauce, tomatoes, salt and pepper. Cook until the mixture comes to a boil. Stir occasionally.

3. Reduce the flame and add the red wine and tomato paste. Simmer the sauce for about 30 minutes stirring occasionally.

4. In a separate large frying pan over high heat add 2 tablespoons olive oil and once the oil is hot add the squid, shrimp and scallops. Cook for about 4 minutes or until the shrimp turn pink. Stir frequently.

5. Add the sea food ready mixture in the tomato sauce prepared in step 3 and stir everything to coat nicely. Add the parsley and basil. 6. Cook the sauce for 3 – 4 minutes or until the sauce begins to sizzle. Pour over your choice of pasta and serve!

25) Honey & Peanut Butter Pasta Sauce

Preparation Time: 10 minutes

Cooking Time: none

Ready In: 10 minutes

Servings: 8

INGREDIENTS:

1/4 cup peanut butter (smooth)

1/4 cup honey

1 tablespoon crunchy peanut butter

2 tablespoons rice vinegar

3 tablespoons soy sauce

1 tablespoon ginger root, minced fresh

2 teaspoons garlic, minced fresh

1 tablespoon red pepper flakes, crushed

1 tablespoon sesame oil

2 tablespoons extra-virgin olive oil

DIRECTIONS:

1. Combine all the ingredients in a small bowl.

2. Pour over your choice of pasta, toss and serve!

26) Bechamel Pasta Sauce

Preparation Time: none

Cooking Time: 20 minutes

Ready In: 20 minutes

Servings: 4

INGREDIENTS:

2 small zucchini (or one large)

1/3 cup diced cooked ham

2 tablespoons freshly grated Parmigiano Reggiano

6 tablespoons unsalted butter

1/2 cup all-purpose flour

4 cups warm whole

Pinch of freshly ground black or white pepper

Pinch of ground nutmeg

1 tablespoon olive oil

Salt and pepper as per taste

DIRECTIONS:

1. Wash and dry the zucchini. Then trim the end and cut in half length-wise. Cut each half length-wise again and then dice into bite-sized pieces.

2. Place a medium sized frying pan over medium heat and add the olive oil to it. Once the oil is hot enough add the zucchini to this and sauté until it turns crisp.

Add the salt and pepper and stir to coat nicely. Remove from heat.

3. Place a medium sized saucepan over medium-low heat and melt about 5 tablespoons butter in it.

4. Add the flour to the melted butter and whisk until the mixture becomes smooth. This should take about 2 minutes and the mixture should be a pale yellow color. While stirring the flour in the butter add the warm milk and stir so that no lumps are formed.

5. Reduce the flame and simmer the mixture until it thickens to a creamy consistency. Take care not to boil the sauce. To test the consistency, coat the back of a wooden spoon with the sauce and run your finger down the middle. If the sauce does not seep back, it is ready.

6. Remove the sauce from the heat and add the salt and pepper. Cover the pan with a tight lid and set aside for about 5 minutes.

7. Mix the ready zucchini in the sauce and also add the dices ham.

8. For best results, mix this sauce with the pasta of your choice and spread in a butter greased 9 x 13 inch baking dish and cover the dish with foil. Bake in a preheated oven at 350 degrees for about 30 minutes and serve hot!

27) Italian Sausage & Basil Pasta Sauce

Preparation Time: none

Cooking Time: 3 hours and 20 minutes

Ready In: 3 hours and 20 minutes

Servings: 6

INGREDIENTS:

1 pound Italian sausage links, sliced

1 1/2 teaspoons dried leaf basil, crumbled

1/4 cup chopped green bell pepper

6 to 8 ounces sliced mushrooms

1/3 cup chopped onion

2 cans tomato paste

2 cans tomatoes, coarsely chopped

3 cans tomato sauce

1/4 teaspoon dried leaf thyme

1 1/2 teaspoons dried leaf oregano, crumbled

1/2 teaspoon dried leaf parsley

1 teaspoon garlic powder

1 1/2 teaspoons sugar

1/2 teaspoon vinegar

2 tablespoons olive oil

1 cup water

Salt and Pepper as per taste

Grated parmesan cheese

DIRECTIONS:

1. Place a large heavy skillet on high heat and place the sausage slices on it. Cook them until they turn brown in color. When done, drain off the excess grease in the skillet.

2. Add olive oil to this and when the oil heats up add the onions, mushrooms and green bell peppers. Cook everything until the onions become tender. Stir frequently.

3. Now add the tomatoes, tomato paste, tomato sauce, basil, parsley, thyme, oregano, garlic powder, sugar, vinegar and water to this and stir to combine everything nicely.

4. Let this sauce cook over medium-low heat for 2 – 3 hours stirring occasionally. If the sauce becomes too thick, add more water and reduce the heat.

5. Add the parmesan cheese just before serving!

28) Bolognese Pasta Sauce

Preparation Time: none

Cooking Time: 8 – 10 hours

Ready In: 8 – 10 hours

Servings: 6

INGREDIENTS:

2 pounds ground beef

3 cans chopped tomatoes, drained

2 cans tomato paste

2 cans tomato sauce

1 medium onion, chopped

8 cloves garlic, minced

2 tablespoons dried oregano

1 tablespoon dried basil

1/3 cup sugar

2 teaspoons dried marjoram

Salt and pepper as per taste

DIRECTIONS:

1. Place a large frying pan over medium heat and cook the beef in it until it turns brown in color.

2. When ready, transfer the beef to a 5 quart slow cooker draining off the excess fat.

3. Now add the tomatoes, tomato paste and sauce, oregano, basil, onions, minced garlic, marjoram and sugar and mix everything nicely.

4. Cover the cooker and let the sauce cook for 8 – 10 hours.

5. Serve over your choice of pasta!

29) Peppercorn Pasta Sauce

Preparation Time: 10 minutes

Cooking Time: 40 minutes

Ready In: 50 minutes

Servings: 2

INGREDIENTS:

1 tablespoon peppercorns, grinded

1 large head of garlic

1 tablespoon all-purpose flour, plus 1 teaspoon extra

2 tablespoons butter

1 1/2 cups milk

1 1/4 teaspoons extra-virgin olive oil

Salt and pepper as per taste

Water

DIRECTIONS:

1. Rinse the garlic head under cool tap water and pat dry with a paper towel. Cut off the upper 1/3 portion of the garlic head and set it aside. Now preheat the oven to 350 degrees F.

2. Pour a little water in a baking dish just enough to cover the bottom of the dish. Brush the bottom 2/3 of the garlic head with the olive oil and keep it head facing up in the baking dish. Place a lid on top of the dish and roast the garlic in the oven for 30 minutes. Remove from oven when done.

3. Place a large saucepan over medium heat and add the butter to it. When butter melts, add the flour, milk, black pepper, salt and sugar to it and stir to combine everything.

4. Boil the sauce and then reduce the heat. Keep cooking the sauce on low heat for 5 – 6 minutes until it thickens. Stir constantly.

5. Peel off the skin from the roasted garlic and crush the garlic up. Add this to the sauce and let it simmer for 1 – 2 minutes.

6. Now add in the peppercorns and simmer for another 2 minutes.

7. Remove it from the heat and after 2 minutes pour over your choice of pasta, Toss and serve!

30) Butter, Herbs & White Wine Pasta Sauce

Preparation Time: none

Cooking Time: 20 minutes

Ready In: 20 minutes

Servings: 2

INGREDIENTS:

1/2 tsp fresh rosemary, chopped

1/2 tsp fresh sage, chopped

1/2 tsp fresh thyme, chopped

1/2 cup Double Blind Pinot Grigio (white wine)

4 tbsp butter, melted

Salt and Pepper as per taste

DIRECTIONS:

1. Place a small saucepan over low heat and melt the butter in it.

2. Add the herbs, salt and pepper and mix everything nicely.

3. Now pour the wine and simmer the sauce for about 15 minutes.

4. Pour over your choice of pasta and serve!

31) Cream, Stock, Cheese & White wine Pasta Sauce

Preparation Time: none

Cooking Time: 25 minutes

Ready In: 25 minutes

Servings: 2

INGREDIENTS:

2 cups heavy cream

1/2 cup chicken stock

1 cup crumbly Gorgonzola cheese

2 tablespoons freshly grated Parmesan cheese

1/2 cup dry white wine

Salt, black pepper and Grated nutmeg as per taste

DIRECTIONS:

1. Place a large saucepan over medium-high heat and add the chicken stock, cream and white wine to it. Stir and let the mix come to a bubble. Now reduce the heat and let it simmer for 15 – 20 minutes or until the sauce has reduced by 1/3.

2.Add the cheeses now and stir until they melt and blend fully with the sauce.

3.Now add the salt, pepper and nutmeg and stir. Serve!

www.ingramcontent.com/pod-product-compliance
Lightning Source LLC
Chambersburg PA
CBHW071437070526
44578CB00001B/122